MAN ON FIRE

BY THOMAS KUNKEL

Man on Fire: The Life and Spirit of Norbert of Xanten

Man in Profile: Joseph Mitchell of *The New Yorker*

Enormous Prayers: A Journey Into the Priesthood

Genius in Disguise: Harold Ross of *The New Yorker*

Letters From The Editor: *The New Yorker*'s Harold Ross (Editor)

Leaving Readers Behind: The Age of Corporate Newspapering
(Editor, with Gene Roberts and Charles Layton)

Breach of Faith: A Crisis of Coverage in the Age of Corporate
Newspapering (Editor, with Gene Roberts)

MAN ON FIRE

The Life and Spirit of Norbert of Xanten

By Thomas Kunkel

St. Norbert College Press
in association with the Center for Norbertine Studies

© Thomas Kunkel 2019

Published by St. Norbert College
in association with the Center for Norbertine Studies

Printed in the United States of America by IngramSpark

ISBN 978-0-9851080-8-3

Library of Congress Control Number 2019901780

Cover image and illustrations by Brother Martin Erspamer, O.S.B.

Book design by Laura Treichel

For my Norbertine colleagues,
who took me in and helped me understand that we are
ever ancient, ever new.

CONTENTS

INTRODUCTION

In 2008, I was named president of St. Norbert College, a vibrant and highly esteemed liberal arts institution in De Pere, Wisconsin, just outside Green Bay. In taking up that role, I also entered into the world of the ancient Premonstratensian order of Catholic priests, brothers and sisters. Though a lifelong Catholic, I didn't know much about the Premonstratensians— or as they are more commonly known, the Norbertines—before I arrived. Soon enough, though, the order would become a big and ennobling part of my life, as it has been ever since.

Norbert of Xanten lived in the late eleventh and early twelfth centuries, and he was an early and headstrong Church reformer. He was also a nobleman, a courtier, a priest, an ascetic, an itinerant preacher, an archbishop, a defender of papal authority and of the sacrament of the Eucharist, a legendary peacemaker and an exemplar of the apostolic way of life. In addition, in the remote woods of northeast France, Norbert would found one of the great clerical orders of the Church— one that has endured, despite wars, plagues, famines, the Protestant Reformation, Napoleonic suppression, Nazism, fascism, communism and Church politics, through nine long centuries to our present time.

Put another way, Norbert led one of the most remarkable lives of saints before or since.

Still, like me before I decamped to De Pere, few American Catholics know St. Norbert or the order he established in Prémontré (hence its official name) in 1120. This lack of familiarity owes primarily to the fact that for most of their history the Norbertines operated almost exclusively in Europe and have had a much smaller footprint in North America than their Jesuit, Benedictine, Franciscan or Dominican counterparts. Beyond that, most of what has been written about Norbert over the years has come from Europe, in languages only infrequently rendered into English. And even when they were, his story was seldom told in a contemporary way.

And there has been one more challenge: For all Norbert's experiences and accomplishments, he was, perhaps first and foremost, a preacher. He lived and persuaded by means of the spoken word, and he left behind virtually no written record. We have no Norbert letters, no epistles, no essays, no personal theology set down for posterity. He left it to others to document and interpret his life, and Norbertine scholars and historians have been doing just that for nearly nine hundred years. But as one would expect, their audience has primarily been an internal and/or academic one.

Over time, as I came to study Norbert's personal story and more deeply appreciate the Norbertine tradition, I began to feel that it would be useful to have a short, modern, English-language version of our patron's life. What I had in mind was a work that could be a first-year book for incoming St. Norbert students, for instance, or for laymen and -women who happen to be interested in the man or his considerable legacy. And that is what I have tried to write here.

Of course, all biography is an exercise in interpretation; it cannot be otherwise. Biographers aim to be as faithful as possible to the "facts" of a subject's life, but in truth that's an impossible and unknowable standard. What has "really" happened in an individual's life is known only to that person—and even then he or she can have little objectivity about the enduring impact of that life.

This interpretive approach is even more necessary the more distant the subject, and with Norbert we are quite distant indeed—nearly a millennium—and so it should be said, especially to my Norbertine friends and colleagues, that to a great extent the man portrayed here is "my" Norbert. I hope you recognize and appreciate him, but yours may well be different.

As I say, this short book does not claim to be an exhaustive history of Norbert, nor is it an academic treatise. I have endeavored to make it readable, relatable, accessible and brisk. As such, I have elected to forgo footnotes (I find those text interruptions nearly lethal to reading for pleasure) and have not cited every arcane publication consulted. A list at the back of the book identifies the key published sources. But in general, where essential points derive uniquely from those sources, I've tried to say as much right there in the text.

As with all biographical undertakings about Norbert of Xanten, the two primary sources are what the Norbertines call *Vita A* and *Vita B*. These are related biographical sketches of

3

Norbert that were set down by his followers in the years soon after his death in Magdeburg, Germany, in 1134. Though both have something of the hagiographic "spin" typical of medieval histories of saints, their near-contemporaneous nature suggests we can likely trust many of the factual details. Indeed, a great deal of what we know about Norbert's personal life, spiritual development and later career comes from the *Vitae*. A third primary source is Herman of Tournai, a noted French abbot and social historian who was a contemporary of Norbert and wrote about him in several important documents.

From a more modern perspective, anyone studying Norbert owes tremendous gratitude to the Rev. Wilfried Grauwen, O. Praem., a prodigious scholar based at Postel Abbey in Belgium. In 1978 Grauwen produced a book-length dissertation on the later stages of Norbert's life and his tenure as archbishop of Magdeburg. He would then spend much of the rest of his scholarly career turning out a series of chapters covering crucial moments in Norbert's earlier life, providing so much of the context that led up to his episcopal appointment.

In the United States, the foremost authority on Norbert is the Rev. Theodore Antry, O. Praem., who belongs to the Norbertine community at Daylesford Abbey in Pennsylvania. He kindly provided me a large number of his own essays and presentations on Norbert and the order, as well as many others from European scholars that he has translated over the years. He was also gracious enough to read the manuscript and offer some appreciated suggestions.

I have relied as well on a number of previously published

Norbert portraits and translations, which are listed at the back of the book.

I wish to gratefully acknowledge the assistance of a number of other Premonstratensians who are authorities on Norbert or particular aspects of his life and legacy. These include the Rev. Herman Janssens of Averbode Abbey in Belgium, as well as his abbot, the Right Rev. Jos Wouters (who later was elected abbot general of the entire Norbertine order); the Rev. Clemens Doelken of Magdeburg; and the Rev. Dominique-Marie Dauzet of Mondaye Abbey in France.

Meantime, I want to especially acknowledge the Rev. Andrew D. Ciferni, O. Praem., also of Daylesford, who until recently was head of the Center for Norbertine Studies at St. Norbert College. Andrew, my friend and a veritable co-conspirator in this project, helped me in countless ways, with his erudition, creativity, network and boundless enthusiasm. I know he joins me in thanking as well Dr. Rosemary Sands, who has succeeded Andrew at the CNS and who was tremendously helpful to me.

Finally, thanks to my De Pere friends and colleagues the Right Rev. Gary Neville, O. Praem., longtime abbot of the De Pere abbey; the Rev. Jay Fostner, O. Praem., vice president of mission and student affairs at St. Norbert College; Dr. Brian Bruess, who succeeded me as president there; and Mike Van Asten, chair of the college's board of trustees.

This book literally could not have been done without their friendship, support and encouragement.

CHAPTER 1

THE SAINT

In the year of Our Lord 1627, on a chill morning in early May, people who lived in and around the Bohemian capital of Prague poured into the streets to witness something extraordinary. A long and glittery procession was coming their way, led off by a lone drummer and eight trumpeters on horseback. They were followed by eighty white-robed Norbertine priests, each bearing a torch, while several dozen other clerics accompanied them, singing and chanting psalms. Then the parade's centerpiece came into view, a magnificent carriage appointed with fine white linen and drawn by six white horses gleaming in the morning sun. The two coachmen guiding the carriage wore richly adorned white livery. Inside, the coach carried a cedar urn plated in silver and gold to symbolize its precious contents. Flanking the carriage were the kingdom's highest-ranking religious officials; people counted more than forty miters, each one atop a bishop or abbot marching in full regalia. And behind them came two hundred additional coaches, stretching as far as the eye could see, ferrying the nobility of Bohemia in their silk finery.

On and on it went, for hours. As the parade passed, the cheering crowds fell in behind it, making the procession ever longer as it slowly approached the city gates. All of Prague thrilled to the sight. It must have seemed to the peasants in particular as if the stained-glass figures from their cathedrals had come to life. Bohemia's civil and ecclesiastical authorities had deliberately conjured a spectacle meant to impress, and they succeeded. No one who saw it would ever forget what would be known as the "translation" (as in the moving from one place to another) of the earthly remains of St. Norbert to Prague.

The procession was merely the beginning of what would be eight full days of celebration-cum-sanctification. In the daylight hours there was nearly nonstop music, popular entertainments and yet more elaborately choreographed spectacles (such as when university students took to boats on the Moldau River to perform an allegorical re-creation of the translation). At night came fireworks. Stitched throughout were Masses and prayer services conducted in Latin, German and Bohemian. And looming above the entire affair, on the high promontory just across the Moldau, were the twin sentinels of Prague Castle and the Norbertine redoubt of Strahov Abbey, nearly adjacent landmarks that silently signified Church-state approval.

Still, for all the pomp, there were a number of curious aspects about the translation of Norbert. To begin with, the founder of the Canons Regular of Prémontré—the Premonstratensians, or more familiarly, Norbertines—had been dead for nearly five hundred years, and through all that time his remains had lain in undisturbed repose in the Church of Our Lady in Magdeburg. Magdeburg was a medieval trading hub situated just west of modern-day Berlin, and was the place where Norbert had presided as archbishop in the last decade of his life. In the long interregnum since, Norbert's reputation, once so prominent throughout much of Christendom, had been considerably eclipsed. Beyond that, in a restless and peripatetic life that would take Norbert from his Rhineland home to the Low Countries to the forests of France to Rome and then back to Germany, with countless stops in between, he never actually came anywhere near Prague, and he'd had only the slimmest of personal connections to the region. Perhaps most significantly, by the early seventeenth century the once heavily Roman Catholic population of Bohemia had been fundamentally transformed by a century of Protestant sway—in particular that of its native son and onetime Catholic priest Jan Hus, a fiery reformer and influential forerunner of Martin Luther. Hus was burned at the stake as a heretic, but as his beliefs took hold among his countrymen and as the so-called Hussites came to outnumber the kingdom's Catholics, they would exact their revenge—burning down monasteries, adulterating many Catholic sacramental and liturgical rituals, and openly mocking still others. Indeed, by the time the authorities were transporting Norbert's remains to Prague, it is estimated that no more than fifteen percent of Bohemians considered themselves Catholic.

But that, in fact, was the point. In recent years the Catholic forces of the Holy Roman Emperor, Ferdinand II, had finally gained the upper hand over the Hussites and instigated their own bloody purge of the Protestant leadership. Now Ferdinand was intent on restoring Catholicism throughout Bohemia—but not entirely at sword-point. "Forced conversion combined with the expulsion of the most obdurate heretics could swell the Church's ranks numerically," explains the religious historian Howard Louthan, "but such harsh tactics would obviously not create loyal Czech Catholics overnight. In response, the Church waged a lengthy cultural campaign to win the loyalty of its new members and restore its tarnished legacy." That is to say, Ferdinand had in mind an early demonstration of trying to win a people's hearts and minds. Louthan calls the tactic "importing piety."

And to this purpose, Norbert—despite being dead for half a millennium—was suddenly very useful. Norbert's adherents had long venerated him for, among other qualities, his devotion to the Eucharist and his staunch defense of Church orthodoxy against heresy. Largely in response to the Reformation, then, the Church recognized this steadfastness by canonizing Norbert in 1582; now his cult was back on the rise. Strahov Abbey, itself one of those Catholic institutions destroyed early in the Hussite Wars, had rebuilt and was helping drive the kingdom's Catholic resurgence. At the same time, the abbot general of the entire Norbertine order was growing increasingly desperate to dislodge Norbert's remains from Magdeburg. That city had become a Protestant stronghold in the Reformation, with the result that Lutherans now were in firm control of the Church of Our Lady, which held Norbert's remains. Worse, they were in effect claiming Norbert—who was, conveniently (for them), an early and prominent Church reformer—as one of their own.

But uprooting Norbert would not be easy, politically or physically. Even as Europe approached the Age of the Enlightenment, saintly connections and relics remained so highly prized that a city's reputation could rise or fall on them. Thus, there was no shortage of principalities or Premonstratensian communities vying for the rehabilitated Norbert. In fact, the previous forty years had seen endless overtures aimed at getting his relics out of Magdeburg. But all had gone for naught; the Lutheran authorities wouldn't be budged. It was only when imperial forces retook control of Magdeburg (in an engagement that was part of the Thirty Years' War) that the opportunity finally presented itself—and the abbot of Strahov, Caspar von Questenberg, seized it. In December of 1626, after having been thwarted several times before, von Questenberg quietly led a small retrieval party to Magdeburg's Church of Our Lady. There, with a regiment of troops literally circling the church while he worked, the abbot opened Norbert's crypt and finally was able to gaze upon his prize. Norbert's bones were intact, along with remnants of his archbishop's miter and vestments. And according to Premonstratensian lore, as von Questenberg examined Norbert's gold ring, it "fell" of its own accord onto the abbot's finger.

The party first moved the remains to a community of Norbertine women (still extant) in Doksany, a remote Czech outpost northwest of Prague. There Norbert would stay through that winter, for safekeeping and to give authorities back in the capital the time they would need to plan their elaborate parade and celebration. Staging a high-profile "homecoming" for sacred relics was hardly a new idea; throughout the tumult of the Reformation, the Church had often mounted such public translations to shore up its support among the people in sectarian lands. But the Hussite separation in Bohemia had been so bloody, and had become so rooted, that both Church and imperial authorities felt an especially impressive display was required. No expense would be spared. Medals were minted to mark the occasion and distributed to the crowds. The town square was festooned with flags, and sixteen specially embroidered banners depicted scenes from Norbert's life. A symbolic arch said to tower sixty feet into the air was constructed in the town square, and on the second day of the celebrations, with the help of a mechanical device, "Saints Wenceslas, Vitus, Ludmila, Procopius, Adalbert and Sigismund descended from the upper story," according to Howard Louthan. "Once on the ground, these six patron saints of the kingdom gestured to an empty throne that was reserved for their new colleague." For good measure, on the eighth and final day of the festivities some six hundred Hussites were hauled to the square to publicly renounce their apostasy (although according to an eyewitness Norbertine account, one obstinate blasphemer apparently paid with "the removal of his legs.")

Norbert's translation had been an unqualified success. Officially declared one of the patron saints of Bohemia, he was re-laid to rest in a specially constructed shrine in a chapel of the abbey church at Strahov.

SO WHAT WAS ALL this fuss about? Who was this Norbert, a man the people of Prague had little emotional or historical kinship with and yet embraced like a conquering hero?

Awash as they were in Norbert tales around the time of the translation, maybe they came to appreciate him as someone who cared not only for their eternal souls but also for their daily lives. Put another way, maybe they considered Norbert one of them.

Well, yes…in a way he *was* one of them—but in so many others he was anything but. In fact he was of noble birth, scion of an influential family that had long controlled much of the fertile territory of the Lower Rhine. A keen young man ostensibly destined for the priesthood, Norbert had the kind of skills and diplomatic qualities that quickly brought him to the attention of Archbishop Frederick of Cologne, and soon thereafter to the court of the Holy Roman Emperor himself, Henry V. And Norbert might have been expected (and content) to remain in those heady circles the rest of his life but for a nagging conscience and a call to give his life over to the Lord—a call so intense that it emboldened him to become one of the earliest critics of clerical corruption. It also coalesced his growing conviction that the people of God should return to the Gospel teachings for their values and to the apostles for their role models—and that he was just the person to tell them as much, face-to-face. So against the backdrop of an apocalyptic fervor (sparked by the arrival of a new millennium and still gripping much of Europe), Norbert began to move from village to village and town to town like a latter-day Elijah admonishing people to make ready for the Lord. And everywhere Norbert went, he ignited in his listeners a spiritual fire. This fervor in turn would lead him to found one of the earliest and most significant religious orders in Church history. And then, in his final act, Norbert would be named archbishop of Magdeburg—a position that would find him risking his life in the name of reform, evangelizing to the far eastern frontier of

Christianity, suppressing heresy, defending the authority of the Rome, and counseling emperors and popes.

And Norbert's character was just as complex and idiosyncratic as his resume. Then as now, we tend to regard our saints as straightforward and uncomplicated, leading lives of undilute goodness. That is seldom true, of course; saints tend to be saints precisely *because* they have overcome their all-too-human failings—as Oscar Wilde quipped, "Every saint has a past." And Norbert was a particularly complicated case in point. A thoroughly medieval man—and a medieval nobleman, with all the socioeconomic entitlement that suggests—Norbert nonetheless led a life that was unpredictable, emotional and often messy. It would yaw from privilege to asceticism and back to privilege. And as it did, Norbert suffered enough internal contradictions to make him seem more like a protagonist from our own age than from his own. As much powerbroker as priest, as much troublemaker as prophet, as determined (many said stubborn, or worse) as he was devout, Norbert was a lifelong provocateur who was far more comfortable asking forgiveness than permission. Though possessed of a nearly unshakeable confidence that at times verged into arrogance, he often experienced self-doubt—and yet he never let that doubt stop him from plunging into his next passion. He was an unassuming man who still managed to cast a long and influential shadow, a genuinely humble man whose humility was nevertheless dwarfed by a personal magnetism so expansive that he left literally hundreds of abbeys and convents, and thousands of devoted acolytes, in his wake.

In an unsentimental assessment, historian Kaspar Elm

captures these contradictions. "Norbert of Xanten wanted more than his time or surroundings allowed," Elm writes. "He strove after a higher goal than anyone in that century could have reached. He wanted to be lord and servant, he wanted to serve emperor and pope, he wanted to preach the word of God and establish or strengthen the domination of the Church, he wanted to follow the naked Christ and at the same time make Christ reign as king. The effort of bridging all these conflicting elements was greater than his strength would allow and greater than the strength that any other saint would have had." But Elm also credits Norbert with a longer-term impact more profound than the young nobleman could ever have imagined. If Norbert's conflicting wants and shifting circumstances might trip him up now and again, his complete conviction and personal rectitude never wavered—and that towering integrity proved a durable inspiration. As Elm points out, one of Norbert's most enduring legacies was paving the way for some of the Church's best-known reformers, who were about to take center stage. "He was the herald of the poverty of St. Francis," Elm writes, "earlier than Dominic he placed the preaching of poverty at the center of his life. More intensely than Bernard he sought to influence the pope in the spirit of the reform of the Church in that time."

Of course, Norbert's other great legacy is the religious order that he established at Prémontré and that came to bear his name—and to carry his story through the centuries into our present day. For now, though, Norbert's journey had come to an end in Prague, more than five hundred miles and five hundred years from where it began.

CHAPTER 2

THE NOBLEMAN

Xanten is a postcard-pretty medieval village tucked into the northwest corner of Germany, just inside its border with the Netherlands, and its existence owes to its location along the mighty River Rhine. Here along the Lower Rhine the land is flat and the water is fleet, wide and bustling. Out past the ancient city walls as you approach the river, the landscape seems as pastoral as it would have been in Norbert's time—except that now it's never more than a few minutes before a coal-laden barge or a container ship whisks past, heading either into the continent or out to the North Sea. The Rhine is the same hardworking highway that made it so strategic to the early Romans.

Xanten is also historically significant as a northern outpost of early Christianity. Late in the third century, a soldier named Victor and several hundred fellow legionnaires who had converted to Christianity were garrisoned there. Ordered to make sacrifices to the Roman gods, they refused and were killed. This mass martyring would result in the village being named "Xanten," or "from the saints"; to this day Xanten is the only city name in Germany that begins with the letter X. It is still dominated by the imposing twin spires of St. Victor Cathedral, just off the town square. Begun in the middle of the thirteenth century, the massive edifice that would replace Norbert's boyhood church would take three centuries to finish and was considered the most important cathedral between Cologne and the North Sea.

No one can say with certainty, but the figure known to history as Norbert of Xanten was just as likely born in Gennep, another medieval village in what is now the far eastern edge of the Netherlands. Gennep is only twenty miles west of Xanten, a distance that at the time would have been an easy horse ride of half a day, or a hard full day on foot. The village lies on the right bank of another of the region's important rivers, the Maas (or the Meuse, to French speakers), and just south of where it intersects with a tributary, the Niers.

Gennep takes its name from the family of nobles that for generations held title on the rich agricultural lands of this region. Their extensive holdings encompassed both Gennep and Xanten, and considerably beyond. In fact, the House of Gennep was one of the most influential in this part of the Holy Roman Empire—and this was the family into which Norbert was born in the latter part of the eleventh century.

The exact year of Norbert's birth is also uncertain. It had traditionally been put around 1080, but more recent scholarship dates it closer to 1075. The boy likely was born in the ancestral castle of his family, a stronghold situated right at the confluence of the Maas and the Niers so as to control all activity on the waterways. (The family also occupied a more formal manor house in Xanten.) His father, Heribert, was the count of Gennep and a blood relation of the imperial family. His mother,

Hedwig, descended from another noble line, from the Laon region of eastern France. Their oldest son, also named Heribert, would inherit his father's title and estate; a third son, Herbert, is said to have died as a young man in battle, in Palestine, in the early days of the Crusades. The middle son they would christen Norbert, meaning "Light of the North." And as was common at the time for a second son in a family of means, Norbert would be destined from a young age for a life in the clergy.

Both Xanten and Gennep were part of the duchy of Lower Lorraine, one of the many disparate states that constituted the Holy Roman Empire. The age was the height of feudalism. In the agrarian-based feudal system, vast estates were controlled by noblemen like Norbert's father, whose authority and property rights derived from the emperor but were generally inheritable. Armies of peasants (known as serfs) worked the farms, woodlands, kitchens, stables, mills, forges and other outposts of these estates and pledged loyalty to their lord; in exchange they received his protection and food and shelter for their families. Over the next few centuries, as the Crusades created busy new trade routes across Europe and into the Middle East, feudalism would give rise to the merchant and guild classes that were the precursors of modern economies. But in the late eleventh century, as had been true for all of civilization, the great majority of people were of the peasant class: illiterate and uneducated, fated to lives of grinding labor and meager prospect.

Not so the young nobleman Norbert; he had been dropped into a life of utter privilege. And like most such princelings he would develop a strong sense of entitlement about things, because he literally *was* entitled to them: the finest fabrics for his clothing, the best available food and wine, the most beautiful horses to ride, even his superior social station. For their part the feudal classes who worked the land, while tacit participants in the social contract, could only hope for overlords who were somewhat benevolent—that they might manifest a bit of *noblesse oblige*, or the idea that having wealth and privilege carried a responsibility to wield that good fortune generously and humanely. Many landholders felt no such compulsion, of course, abusing their serfs in ways akin to slaveholders in the American South centuries later. But other lords were more principled. We cannot know beyond contradiction how the count of Gennep treated his serfs. But given the (admittedly sketchy) reports that have come to us from Norbert's youth, and considering the core values that we know he carried away from his own upbringing, it is reasonable to suppose that life in the fields around Gennep and Xanten was, for those times, comparatively tolerable.

Out in the wider world, though, things were anything but sanguine. Momentous forces were converging that soon enough would redirect the history of both Europe and the Catholic Church—changes that would shape the younger Norbert, and that the older Norbert would himself help shape.

THE GREAT FRENCH writer-philosopher of the Enlightenment, Voltaire, famously quipped, "The Holy Roman Empire was neither holy, nor Roman, nor an empire." True enough. But it *was* formidable, a geopolitical powerhouse that had emerged from the rubble of the old Roman empire and that managed to endure in one form or another into the early nineteenth century. While its boundaries were ever-shifting, the Holy Roman Empire essentially comprised a huge swath of central Europe, including the kingdoms of Germany, Bohemia (the modern Czech Republic and Slovakia, as well as western Poland), Burgundy (eastern France and much of modern Switzerland) and northern Italy. In political terms, however, it was a ragged and fractious confederation involving hundreds of principalities, city-states, duchies and other quasi-independent entities. Loyalty to empire and other common interests (Catholicity, mutual defense) bonded them, but fitfully so. Alliances were constantly being formed and dissolved among them, intrigues hatched and exposed. Power was the only currency that truly mattered.

Over the centuries the empire had derived much of its authority from its symbiotic relationship with the Catholic Church. The alliance afforded the pope protection and, in general, the patronage of affiliated rulers. The empire unquestionably benefited from the arrangement as well. Having the pope's (in effect, God's) imprimatur to rule was seen as essential to the emperor's legitimacy. But there were far more prosaic considerations at work, too. In that pre-Gutenberg age, clerics were among the few people with formal educations. From kings to counts, secular authorities naturally came to rely on these religious personages for recordkeeping, correspondence, mediation of disputes, and the other nuts and bolts of administration. (The words "clergy" and "clerk" stem from the same Latin root.) Across the medieval world, Church and empire became so bound up with one another that they were like two threads stitched into the same tapestry. In any case, the serf in the field would have made no distinction between the two institutions; to him, lords and priests both belonged to the ruling class, and it didn't really matter if they were controlling his taxes or his soul.

The political demands of imperial rule only tightened this Church-state nexus. Since emperors and kings needed deputies whose loyalty could be counted on (including in their most influential clerical postings), they increasingly took to selecting the bishops and abbots in their realms themselves. In time this practice became the rule. In this way, noblemen were simultaneously becoming princes of the Church—just as churchmen were now being appointed lords and vassals, gaining not only exalted new titles but the tremendous wealth and political clout that often came with them. Though canon law reserved exclusively to Rome the right to appoint bishops (known as "investiture"), the Church of the Middle Ages had largely acquiesced to this arrangement—the king appoints, the pope anoints—because it had tended to work for all parties and it amortized political influence. However, by the middle of the eleventh century, with reformers ascendant in the Church, this ceding of episcopal investiture was increasingly seen as a grave infringement on papal authority. Investiture was starting to become a source of great tension for Rome, especially as to its enthusiastic practice across Germany.

That tension built until reaching a flashpoint in the latter half of the eleventh century. The emperor during this period,

Henry IV, had little use for religion in general and the papacy in particular. He had inherited his father's crown at the tender age of six, and as he grew into young adulthood he was far more concerned with staving off usurpers than with his standing with the Church. As he fought to reclaim the power that had leached away during his youth, Henry only became more autocratic in his investiture practices, and indeed his true aim was to make even the pope, in time, subservient to himself.

Then in 1073, with Henry still a temperamental young man in his twenties, the throne of St. Peter's came to be occupied by one of the great reformers in Church history. An Italian named Hildebrand, he was said to be of humble birth (the son of a blacksmith, some had it). He would reign as Pope Gregory VII. Much older than Henry, the new pope had flourished amid decades of Church infighting; he was not easily cowed. It seemed a foregone conclusion that these two imposing and stubborn figures would come to blows, and soon enough they did.

But Gregory had inherited other problems besides an antagonistic emperor. As it entered its second millennium, the Church was experiencing great internal ferment. Of course, the institution ostensibly responsible for the souls of most of the Western world held inestimable power; eternal damnation was a sobering prospect, even for kings. Yet the Church's spiritual character was at a low ebb. Indeed, in many ways the Roman Catholic Church of this period looked less like the institution we know today than it did just another European medieval state— and a state with too many leaders who had succumbed to the same worldly temptations, intrigues and moral compromising as

23

their secular counterparts. Over time, highly questionable, even corrupt, practices had been allowed to take root. A particularly nefarious example was simony, the graft-like practice where bishoprics and other Church offices were essentially for sale, or where priests took money in exchange for such intangibles as the blessings of the Holy Spirit. (In this way simony was a cousin to the abusive market in indulgences that would later help spark the Reformation.) Another contentious issue for the Church was whether its priests should be required to be unmarried and celibate. To this point in Church history, priests could marry and many did. But even those who didn't tended not to be celibate; priests commonly maintained mistresses, even in their households. Beyond its moral implications, the marriage-celibacy issue had maddeningly practical consequences for the Church: where priests had families, parish goods and property tended to vanish, either through inheritance or straightforward theft.

Then there was the march of Islam. The Islamic faith arose on the Arabian peninsula in the seventh century. But by this point its caliphates had taken Jerusalem and the Holy Land, spread across the northern tier of Africa and crossed the Mediterranean to occupy the Iberian territories. Indeed, around the time of Norbert's birth Western armies were on their way to Jerusalem—after insistent urging from Rome—marking the start of the Crusades. Of course, what the Western powers hoped would be a hasty retaking of the Holy Land instead became a bloody slog of several centuries' duration—one that sowed hatreds so deep they are shaping global events to this day.

As Gregory began his papacy, then, his Church found itself

battling on two fronts: internally, for its own soul, and externally, to hang onto what it considered its divinely received authority.

The headstrong new pontiff took to both fights with a reformer's zeal. Having extended some initial but fruitless diplomatic overtures to Henry, Gregory suddenly issued a breathtaking decree setting forth twenty-seven principles and prerogatives of papal authority, among them: that "the Roman Church was founded by God alone"; that only the pope can dismiss and install bishops; that he cannot be judged by any other man; that he has the power to depose emperors; and that, crucially, he has the further power "to absolve subjects from their oath of fealty to unjust men." Thus was the gauntlet thrown down before Henry. These principles, says historian Johannes Fried, "stressed the monarchical exclusivity of the pope and, as a consequence, the subservience and unquestioning obedience of the entire Church, namely all prelates and lay people including the king."

Now, asserting those principles was one thing. Gregory somehow had to make them stick, and his fight with Henry was about to explode into what became known as the Investiture Controversy—a deceptively antiseptic name for such an emotional, high-stakes standoff.

Henry answered the pope's provocation in kind: he withdrew imperial support of the Church and even challenged Gregory's papal legitimacy. Gregory's response to this was quick, and shocking to the Christian world. He excommunicated Henry—and more, he released Henry's lords from their allegiance to him. The turn of events emboldened Henry's old enemies in Germany, and he quickly realized he had overreached.

Deciding he must restore himself to the pope's good graces, the young emperor abased himself to meet with Gregory in the northern Italian town of Canossa. There, in a highly symbolic act, he donned a hair shirt and stood barefoot in the snow, asking (and receiving) forgiveness. But this "walk to Canossa" had been a cynical gesture; soon enough Henry resumed his fight with Rome, even going so far as to install an antipope of his own. In response to that, Gregory excommunicated Henry a second time—and later, for good measure, a third.

The high-stakes drama that was the Investiture Controversy would play out over many years in many venues. It would actually outlive both Henry and Gregory, and Henry's son would inherit the battle and wage it even more ruthlessly. But eventually Rome would prevail in the right to appoint bishops, and by the time Gregory died in 1085 he had brought about profound change, both within the Church—he banned clerical marriage, for instance, and set the stage for enforcement of priestly celibacy—and without. Indeed, his papacy would come to be regarded as a watershed event in European history, and he built the foundation for the modern Catholic Church. "All these [twenty-seven] guiding principles have precursors and a long history," Fried writes of Gregory's audacious assertion of papal prerogative, "and yet the brusque manner in which Gregory formulated them and the consistency with which he subjugated all the institutions of the Church to them and imposed his new order indicate that his pontificate was a turning point in the history of the papacy and of the Catholic Church. 'The Roman Church opens and closes the Gates of Heaven to whomsoever it chooses according to its unique privilege,' is another principle stated elsewhere, but fully in keeping with Gregory's edicts. Rarely have so few words summed up in its entirety the change from one era to another and, moreover, one of the greatest revolutions in European history."

As it happens, Norbert would come to know Henry V personally and even find himself an eyewitness to the brute, bare-knuckle politics of the investiture fight. That experience, in fact, would be a major factor in Norbert's own spiritual evolution and reckoning. Yet as he lay as an infant in his mother's cradle, it was not remotely clear how any of this would turn out.

COMING OF AGE in and around Xanten, Norbert was, as one biographer puts it, "a real Rhinelander," unquestionably a product of his people's foursquare and practical traits. Just as the boy would come to know every bend in his home river, he knew equally well the mystical tales of the Lorelei and the rich, Rhine-inspired folklore that still courses deeply through the German soul. He could recite the story of brave Victor and his legionnaire-saints, which must surely have inspired a young man bound for the clergy. And he was mesmerized by the liturgies and sacramental rituals as he experienced them in the cathedral.

It was at the cathedral too where Norbert would have received his first, and most formational, studies. The church maintained a "collegiate school" in which the resident clerics instructed the region's boys who had been identified for religious development. Norbert likely began this instruction around age eight. All lessons were conducted in Latin and the curriculum was formed along the classic model inherited from the Romans—the *trivium* and the *quadrivium*. The first subjects Norbert was exposed to, covered in the *trivium*, were grammar (via the writings of Ovid and Cicero and Virgil); rhetoric, with a particular emphasis on written communication; and logic. Then came the more scientifically oriented *quadrivium*—arithmetic (including mastery of an abacus or counting instrument of some type); Euclidean geometry; astronomy; and music (less an appreciation than analysis of music's mathematical structure). Of course, as the school's main purpose was cultivating future priests, all Norbert's classes were taught in a scriptural context. The teachings of St. Augustine figured especially prominently in this early theological training. The master opened his precious text (each book having been painstakingly created by a monk's steady hand) and read aloud, until his young charges had committed the material to memory.

Norbert was an adept student, and after his initial instruction at Xanten he would have been sent on for advanced studies (and additional polishing) to an imperial school—most likely in the major center of Cologne, some eighty miles upriver. It is said he better appreciated the more "applied" aspects of his studies than their intellectual underpinnings; he was never destined to be a philosopher. But the one quality every observer remarked on, even from his youth, was Norbert's extraordinary speaking skill. He was exceedingly articulate, even eloquent, and spoke in a manner that people invariably found engaging.

As he became a young man, Norbert was somewhat taller than his peers and had the erect carriage that one might expect given his social rank. He was considered handsome, with a rose-ate countenance that radiated vitality. In short, he cut a striking figure, all the more so for his demeanor of easy confidence—the type of person we might say possesses natural leadership. Even as a boy it was apparent that he could be headstrong and tended to want what he wanted; some biographers suggest he was spoiled by his well-intended parents. Yet they are also in agreement that Norbert had an open and appealing nature, that he genuinely gravitated to other people and that they reciprocat-ed his warmth. And it seems clear that this quality transcended mere friendliness. Norbert had an unusually pronounced gift of empathy. According to *Vita B*, the young Norbert "was pleasing to everyone and open to all," effortlessly adapting to any situ-ation and putting people at ease, whoever they were. He was said to be "great among the great, slight among the unimport-ant, illustrious among the nobles, less than cultured among the ignoble, eloquent among the educated and foolish among the unlearned. To all he showed himself as lovable."

With a first-class education, with a confident, outgoing per-sonality and a nobleman's pedigree, Norbert quickly became a prominent personage—someone to know. He emerged from his formal studies firmly grounded in Latin, conversant in litera-ture and scripture, more than competent in the administrative arts, and with a unique gift for speech. Which is to say, he had acquired the skills and perspective a young man would need to be a successful cleric—or, for that matter, courtier.

CHAPTER 3

THE SEEKER

As medieval cities grew, the Church evolved with them. One such development was the emergence of collegiate churches, including the church in Xanten. These institutions were served by priests, deacons and subdeacons—collectively known as canons—who were organized into chapters. Canons were responsible for conducting their church's liturgies and sacramental rites, educating prospective priests and the children of nobles, and otherwise performing the myriad duties expected of the city's spiritual and social hub. (Xanten's collegiate church, at St. Victor's, was established in the early eleventh century.) Collegiate churches were typically sponsored by the nobles of the region, who often also funded prebends, or lifetime stipends, to support particular clergy. By Norbert's time Rome already had made some initial efforts to reshape these church-based chapters more along the lines of true religious communities, such as the Benedictines and Cistercians. These pioneering communities were another sign of Church evolution and reform; their members committed to living together and following a formal rule. But the attempts to remake secular canons in that image had met with only middling success, so at chapters like that at Xanten the canons might pray together and collaborate on church operational matters, but they tended to live apart and evinced little spiritual cohesion. Individual canons fortunate enough to have prebends were as likely to be committed to their positions for the financial security as for any vocational calling.

Norbert would have been around age twenty when he concluded his formal studies, at which point he returned to Xanten and took up a position at the St. Victor chapter as a subdeacon. The rank no longer exists in the Church, but in the Middle Ages subdeacons were busy functionaries in the daily routine of the church. As the name implies, they assisted priests and deacons in doing most anything (short of the ordained canons' sacramentally prescribed duties) that needed to be done, from the preparations for a High Mass to the singing of the daily office (the chapter's communal chanting of prayers according to the Liturgy of the Hours).

Subdeacons were under no obligation to go on to the diaconate or the priesthood, and in fact many did not. They could keep their personal possessions, and they were not required to be celibate. Thus certain subdeacons were perfectly content with their station, while others had every expectation of continuing up the clerical ladder. Norbert, by joining the Xanten chapter, received the prebend that his family would have established years before. With that stipend, and presumably still able to access some family resources, Norbert was the unusual canon who had no financial worries.

So it was that Norbert settled into his structured new life. Part of it unquestionably appealed to him, especially the majestic beauty of an elaborately staged liturgy or holy-day observance. Still, for a person as inherently restless and worldly as Norbert, this new existence increasingly felt pretty much the opposite— provincial and prosaic. Now formally connected to the Church, he didn't seem to hold any real clerical ambition; certainly the young man who had trained so long for the priesthood never seemed particularly enthused about actually becoming a priest. And we have indications that he didn't take his duties especially seriously; for instance, on occasion he was known to pay other subdeacons to cover his duties for him.

Norbert was one of those canons for whom the collegiate church seems to have been more a point of intersection than a home, an indifferent arrangement made possible by his financial independence and the fish-nor-fowl nature of a subdiaconate. In any event he blithely carried on with the same life of pleasure he'd led prior to his chapter appointment. He is uniformly described during this period as a self-indulgent young man who liked good company and a good time. It is too strong to describe him as a wastrel or a libertine, and we are given no evidence that he engaged in the kinds of carnal adventures that, say, St. Augustine was obliged to confess. But neither is there any reason to imagine that he didn't have the same sexual experiences of other young men of means. In short, the portrait we have of Norbert in his twenties (and probably well into his thirties) is of a likeable if somewhat spoiled hedonist who lacked any spiritual direction or sense of purpose. Norbert, says the Norbertine writer Dino suor Santa, "wastes his best years in search of material satisfactions; his very membership in the chapter of Xanten favors his ambition—this rich prebend, in addition to his many other riches, offers him greater possibilities for amusement." Or in the cryptic yet intriguing words of *Vita B*, "He denied himself nothing and left nothing that he desired untried."

That said, it was also true that Norbert's infectious spirit was one of the reasons he remained widely popular. He had an open heart, and he was equally up for a lively debate about literature (he was as well read as he was well spoken) or a convivial evening over wine. He had a higher intelligence and more of an aura of sophistication than his modest clerical station would suggest; then again, everyone for miles around knew his pedigree. But they also knew him for his lack of commitment and his restlessness, and *Vita B* suggests this latter quality especially was coming to the fore. "He had no time for piety and quiet," it tells us. "He was a slave to unrest and impatience." Norbert was unsettled—but hardly unambitious.

It was not especially surprising, then, that after Norbert spent some appropriate amount of time at Xanten he was summoned to the court of Archbishop Frederick in Cologne. Frederick, a loyal ally of the emperor, was one of the most powerful figures in the northern reaches of the empire, and Norbert was invited to become one of his chaplains. Though the timing of the move is unclear, Norbert was probably in his late twenties or early thirties. The provost of the Xanten chapter, Norbert's superior, would have had to authorize the move, and it's quite possible he even lobbied the archbishop on Norbert's behalf. Still, Norbert would have been known to Frederick already, because of his family and political connections, and from his time studying in Cologne.

With this singular opportunity, Norbert finally *was* moving toward some goal, and one that would genuinely excite him. It would also put his education to fuller use, albeit more for political purposes than for the clerical ones his parents presumed for him decades earlier. He gladly traded the rather sleepy environs of Xanten for the buzzing activity and "worldly spirit," as one biographer calls it, of the archbishop's court in Cologne, with its steady comings and goings of princes and bishops, ambassadors and abbots. Heady stuff for a striving young man who was on his way.

"The chaplains of a bishop constituted a small group of his permanent companions," explains Belgian Norbertine and scholar of the order Wilfried Grauwen. "Just as the secular lords were always surrounded by a group of noblemen, so a bishop, who himself in most cases was a nobleman, was at all times surrounded by a number of clerics." Originally a chaplain's posting was entirely ecclesiastical in nature, as these officials handled all the religious duties and ceremonial pomp attendant to the archbishop's office. But in time, with the continuing integration of nobility with high clergy, chaplains became political legates too. Frederick surely expected his chaplains to possess political skill and finesse, qualities they would only cultivate and sharpen in the service of their bishop-liege. It all made for an indelible apprenticeship for Norbert, who watched carefully how Frederick meshed the twin demands of politics and religion. Norbert "must have known his lord and master the archbishop intimately," says Grauwen. "He lived together with him for some time day and night, and he perhaps accompanied him on his journeys." Given such an executive education, it's easy to see why a chaplaincy was considered a fast track to an episcopal seat of one's own. (At the time, as we have seen, one need not be ordained to become a bishop.)

Norbert would hold this chaplaincy for a number of years, gaining in Frederick's favor and thus in personal stature. He was so successful, in fact, that in time he began focusing on his next step up—as Grauwen puts it, "penetrating into the court of Emperor Henry V."

RULER OF THE HOLY Roman Empire, Henry V ascended to his throne in 1106 after having essentially chased his father out of it. His court was based in Magdeburg, but the king of so vast a dominion was often on the move, the better to be seen by his subjects and, maybe more important, keep an eye on *them*. Not long into Henry's reign—the particulars, as with so much of Norbert's earlier life, are unknown—the archbishop's chaplain climbed another rung by joining the imperial traveling court. Such a leap would not have been possible without Frederick's blessing, though the archbishop no doubt benefited as well from having one of his top aides—Norbert kept his Cologne chaplaincy—doing double duty with the emperor.

In Henry's court Norbert worked in the chancery office, which afforded him another level of experience in the drafting of charters and other important state documents. His main attachment, however, was to the royal chapel, which mounted the sumptuous liturgies that were centerpieces of court life and a powerful symbol of the emperor's divine right to rule. In fact, every aspect of the imperial court was opulent. Norbert was immersed in a world that combined what he liked most about his clerical side (the ceremony and enduring mystery of the rituals) with the finest of secular pleasures. Surrounded by immense wealth, incessant politics and intellectual ferment, Norbert loved everything about the court life. Maybe too much. *Vita B* says of him at this point, "He was...a renowned inhabitant of Babylon," invoking the scriptural shorthand for unchecked hedonism. Of course, the *Vitae* authors' rebuking tone no doubt traced back to Norbert himself, who later in life would have emphasized the profligacy of his former self—perhaps to an exaggerated degree—in persuading listeners how even the most dedicated sinner can change. But it's also true that at a time of emergent Church reform, many observers would have disapproved of Norbert being so ensconced with a man who symbolized papal disobedience. "Babylon? It is undoubtedly a little strong," writes French Norbertine and historian Dominique-Marie Dauzet, "but it must be said that in the eyes of the reformers of the Church, the court of Emperor Henry V of Germany was not a commendable place."

Indeed, Henry was still locked in his fight with Church leaders over the right to name his own bishops, even as Rome stubbornly continued to reserve that prerogative for itself. But Henry also wished to be crowned emperor by the pope, so he decided a "goodwill" overture might be in order. In early 1110 he announced he would march to Rome. The pope at this time was a former monk, Paschal II, a holy man but politically ill-suited to his new role. In addition to the hoped-for coronation, the march would permit Henry to consolidate his authority in the southern regions of his realm, especially Italy. And maybe he could secure at least some concessions from the pontiff as to investiture.

That fall, then, Henry gathered tens of thousands of soldiers and a huge retinue of lords, bishops, chancellors and other courtiers for his arduous trek through the Alps and on to Rome. Frederick, probably the highest-ranking cleric in the imperial entourage, went ahead and met the emperor there. And according to an account years later by the monk Herman of Tournai, so did Norbert.

Just ahead of the emperor's arrival, Henry and Paschal came to a preliminary understanding. Paschal had suggested a startling, if naive, quid pro quo. Henry would renounce the right to investiture, and in return the pope would crown him as emperor and insist that all the bishops in the empire return to Henry their titles, properties and other worldly goods. Henry agreed, but cynically; he knew his bishops would never accept Paschal's terms. In essence, he tricked the pope. And indeed, when Paschal announced the plan—St. Peter's being filled at the time with imperial troops—Henry's bishops, enraged at the sudden prospect of losing both face and fortune, shouted him down. Chaos ensured. Paschal, refusing to crown Henry, was removed from his seat and forcibly detained for two months before he made a deal for his release. Soon after, he would crown Henry as emperor and, under duress, recognize Henry's right to choose his bishops.

Now, tradition has it that Norbert was so appalled at Paschal's humiliation—not to mention the implication of Norbert's own involvement in the sordid affair—that he went to the pontiff to seek his forgiveness. This account also derives from Herman of Tournai, who wrote that "when [Norbert] saw the wickedness of his lord, the king…he prostrated himself at the feet of the pope" and received absolution from him.

More recent scholarship raises considerable doubt whether Norbert—a high official in Henry's court, after all, and still ambitious—would have made such an overt and conciliatory gesture toward Paschal and, in effect, committed political suicide. Wilfried Grauwen goes even further, saying it's a fair question whether Norbert participated in the Rome trip at all. He points out that Herman of Tournai is literally the only historical source to place Norbert there, and his account was written many years after the fact and based on hearsay. On the other hand, since there were numerous courtiers in Henry's retinue, it is not especially surprising that Norbert's name doesn't turn up in primary documents or contemporaneous accounts of the march. So it is not unreasonable to believe that Norbert *was* present.

And even if Norbert did not actually go to Paschal in mortification, it's also not unreasonable to think that witnessing Henry's unapologetic abuse of the pope left Norbert profoundly shaken. It might well have prompted him to wonder where his core allegiances lay: to the ruler of his state or the ruler of his faith? Certainly Herman of Tournai regarded it as a turning point in Norbert's life, and many modern commentators have likewise described that traumatic experience in Rome as a kind of "first conversion." When Henry's entourage left for home in the spring of 1111, Norbert, they say, may already have begun a different, and more spiritual, journey.

This notion is reinforced by another watershed event in Norbert's life—and another whose authenticity is debated. It occurred two years after the confrontation in Rome. A vacancy had opened up in the bishopric of Cambrai, a large, prosperous diocese in what is now northern France. Norbertine lore has it that Henry offered the position to his dutiful courtier from Xanten, but that Norbert turned him down. As such a rejection would have been almost unthinkable, especially for a man who seems to have spent much of his adult life angling for just such a sinecure, Norbert's biographers tend to hold up this decision as evidence that he was reassessing his fealty to the emperor. After exhaustive scouring of the available record, Grauwen again raises questions about the episode as it has come down to us. Given Norbert's position and his upward career arc in two courts, it's certainly feasible that he would have been considered for the bishopric, Grauwen writes. But the historian just doesn't find concrete proof that it was actually offered to him.

Then again, we don't know that it wasn't. And if it was, Norbert might have refused for less noble reasons than conscience. Perhaps he considered Cambrai too far away or unfamiliar. Or maybe Norbert declined because he was already discerning a path for himself that headed in a different direction—toward preaching, say, as opposed to Church administration. Either way, Grauwen's overriding point is that many of the key anecdotes in

Norbert's commonly accepted life story, as with those of virtually all early saints, must be read with a dose of skepticism, because their hagiographers were far less interested in the actual facts of those lives than in the moral lessons to be drawn from them.

As for this particular anecdote, its source, ironically, is the man who actually *did* become bishop of Cambrai. Named Burchard, he was a longtime friend and fellow courtier of Norbert. While traveling some years later, the bishop came across Norbert by chance when the latter was an itinerant preacher and in very reduced circumstances. Astonished by Norbert's ragged clothing and frail, neglected appearance, Burchard told his assistant, "This man whom you see was brought up with me in the court of the king, a man noble and abounding in delights to such a degree that he refused my bishopric when it was offered to him." Burchard's aide was a priest named Hugh of Fosse, who would later succumb to Norbert's missionary zeal, join him in establishing Prémontré and become his second-in-command. And since Hugh almost certainly informed the *Vitae* stories, there is little reason to doubt what Burchard said at the time. The only question is whether he said it out of respect for his haggard-looking friend, or sympathy, or sadness—or maybe all three. But whether Henry in fact offered Norbert the seat of Cambrai is probably unknowable.

What seems beyond dispute, though, is that Norbert was by now in the midst of serious introspection. Further evidence comes from his attendance at a major conference on Church reform, which was sponsored by the pope and held in Cologne over Easter of 1115. Rome had revoked Henry's extorted right

of investiture, and a number of bishops had subsequently pronounced the emperor excommunicated. His political support in
general was crumbling; even his former ally Archbishop Frederick had recently turned against him. And at the papal conference in Frederick's archdiocesan seat, the retaking of investiture
rights was just one of many reform topics under discussion. The
importance of the conference can be inferred from the fact that
three future popes were there—the men who would become
Gelasius II, Callixtus II and Honorius II. Norbert was undoubtedly influenced by the people he was seeing and the ideas he was
hearing. Change was in the air.

NOT LONG AFTER THE Cologne conference, in late
spring or early summer, Norbert was riding on horseback to the
village of Vreden, about twenty miles northeast of Xanten. He
was accompanied by a lone servant, and they were enjoying a
pleasantly uneventful journey on a sunny afternoon. Then the
sky grew ominous. A storm blew up so quickly and violently that
the servant implored his lord to seek shelter. But as they were in
the woods with no immediate refuge available, Norbert decided
to push ahead despite the driving wind and rain.

Suddenly a bolt of lightning hit the ground before them,
"opening it to the depth of a man's height," reports *Vita A*, and
emitting a foul, sulfuric odor. Thrown from his mount, Norbert
lay unconscious for a long time. Then, as he gradually came
to, he was jarred again—this time by a disembodied voice

speaking to him. "Turn from evil and do good," it said—a passage Norbert would have recognized from the thirty-fourth Psalm. "Seek peace and pursue it."

With that, Norbert recovered his horse to return home— and to redirect his life as fully and completely as any other saint that we know of.

What has come to be known as Norbert's "conversion" experience in the Vreden woods is the central event in the Norbert story. The sole source for it are the *Vitae*, which strongly suggests that this tale comes to us from Norbert's own recounting of it to his early followers—a scene one can easily imagine in the ghostly woods of Prémontré, as the leader holds them rapt with his vivid description of divine intervention. Of course, with no other historical corroboration of this account, there is once again no way to know whether this terrifying encounter actually happened—or in any case, happened in the way legend has it. Conversion experiences are common enough in the lives of the saints, nor was Norbert's the first to explicitly echo St. Paul's own violent interdiction on the road to Damascus.

Whatever the particulars, it is likely that Norbert did experience *some* kind of catalyzing event, a trigger powerful enough to finally move his heart. And in truth, it scarcely matters what that event was. One of the problems with being tethered to such a bold story is that Norbertine followers through the centuries have tended to make their man a kind of binary proposition— one day Norbert was still going about his sinning and self-indulgent ways, and the next, post-storm, he was our saint. But that explanation doesn't give Norbert the human being enough credit. Norbertine scholars all agree that the decision to redirect his life to God didn't stem from a single incident, no matter how traumatic or meteorologically enhanced. Rather, it was the culmination of an ongoing and deliberate discernment about what he believed, and why—and what he was going to do about that sacred conviction for the remainder of his life.

And that was no trivial question, spiritually or actuarially. Even nine centuries later, when people speak of Norbert's conversion, he is typically characterized as a callow young man still figuring out his life's course, as callow young men eventually will. But even if you assume for him a birth date of 1080, which until recently was thought to be the case, Norbert would have been in his middle thirties when he made that fateful ride to Vreden. And more likely he was closer to forty. Which means that Norbert, for his time, was already a middle-aged man. His most energetic years presumably were behind him, and as for going forward, well, most middle-aged people (then as now) aren't interested in major life changes. But then again, Norbert was assuredly not "most people." Never satisfied, never sitting still, he was fully capable of seeking a new path—and once committed, he wanted to get started.

"When we look at the basic meaning of the word 'conversion,' a 'turning away from something' or a 'turning toward something,' and we look back at the words Norbert heard during his ride to Vreden ('Turn away from evil and do good; seek peace and pursue it') we see that Norbert did just that very thing," explains Norbertine and historian Theodore Antry. "He turned from his former life, whether it was in fact evil or merely lax, and he began to follow Christ as his only goal. *Christo solo duce*—Christ was his only guide."

So Norbert is called by God—but to what purpose? To try to find out, he abruptly took leave of Henry's court and made a pilgrimage to one of the region's best-known holy places, a Benedictine abbey in Siegburg, south of Cologne. Abbot Conon of Siegburg offered his tutelage and Norbert immersed himself in a regimen of scriptural study, private prayer, theological dialogue and reflection. Beneath his silk clothing he took to wearing a hair shirt. This intense introspection went on for months, and when it was done Norbert had arrived at a decision: he would become a priest after all. With Conon's support, he returned to Cologne to ask his longtime patron, Archbishop Frederick, for ordination.

Frederick was pleased—and surprised. By now he knew Norbert as well as anyone, and he had seen how many times his chaplain had deflected invitations to holy orders. But what Norbert raised next truly took Frederick aback—he asked to be ordained both a deacon and priest *on the same day*. The idea was almost unheard of, and in any case such a contravention of canon law required a special dispensation. Frederick insisted Norbert explain his rash request.

At this, Norbert related it all—the event in the Vreden woods, his process of discernment with Conon at Siegburg, even pulling back the silk from his shoulder to reveal the hair shirt. The archbishop, grasping Norbert's evident seriousness and certainly mindful of his stubbornness, began to see. Still, he asked one last time: Why such a hurry? To which Norbert replied,

"As the Gospel says, you will understand later." An American Norbertine abbot, Benjamin Mackin, would note many centuries later that Norbert's out-of-the-blue insistence on simultaneous ordinations was just another sign of the hardheaded zeal that would mark the rest of his life. "Once he has set his mind to something," writes Mackin, "nothing stands in his way."

A week or so before Christmas Day, 1115, Norbert was ordained at the cathedral in Cologne. Before donning his priestly vestments, Norbert stood before the assembly in his most dazzling lay clothing. Then, as he removed a luxurious fur mantle, his servant brought up a tunic of lambskin, a coarse garment of the type worn by pilgrims and even hermits. Norbert put it on. A ripple of astonishment went through the pews. The symbolic gesture was as clear as it was forceful: Norbert had changed. A shepherd was ready to lead his flock.

After the ordination, Norbert slipped away and returned to Siegburg Abbey and to Conon. He undertook another retreat, this one of (more symbolism) forty days' duration, to continue his spiritual cleansing and prepare himself for his new duties at Xanten. And it was a particularly daunting challenge that awaited him there: He was to try to persuade his colleagues to reform their chapter into a true religious community, one comporting with the Church's explicit guidelines and expectations.

The Mass Norbert celebrated to mark his homecoming seems to have been a joyous occasion, and the service passed smoothly enough until after the Gospel reading. At that point Norbert surprised his colleagues by turning to them and doing something not normally done in this situation—he delivered a sermon. And not just any sermon. He spoke forcefully of the many temptations the world puts before us and cautioned that we not succumb to them lest we be separated from our God. Go and sin no more. Further, while the cathedral was full of friends and family, it was obvious to all that Norbert was directing his message squarely at his clerical brethren. The canons looked to one another in astonishment. How was it that their friend Norbert, of all people, was lecturing them on sin and self-indulgence? Was this some joke?

It was not. At their chapter meeting the very next day, Norbert bore down in the same scolding vein. He read the Church's directives about how secular canons should live and insisted they begin observing the rule. The day after that he did it again—though this time he enumerated specific violations of the rule, and he singled out offending canons by name.

Norbert's old colleagues were confused at first, then insulted, and then, finally, angry. They regarded Norbert as patronizing and hypocritical. "They're suddenly confronted by this neo-convert who himself has been no paragon of virtue," writes Mackin. "He stands before them to tell them what *they* should do. You could naturally expect that they would turn him out." Indeed, after several weeks of this persistent fault-finding they had had enough. According to the *Vitae*, the end came when one young colleague confronted Norbert and spat in his face.

Chastened, Norbert withdrew. Realizing that he was defeated, he determined to leave Xanten. But to where? And to what end?

CHAPTER 4

THE WANDERPREDIGER

If self-awareness wasn't one of Norbert's more pronounced traits, he surely had enough of it to understand why he'd run into such a wall of antagonism from his former colleagues in Xanten. But his far more likely takeaway from that debacle was this: that trying to change the Church from inside its clerical hierarchy might not have been what God had in mind for him when he so rudely unhorsed him on the road to Vreden. Maybe, it seems, he was destined to be the outsider. Norbert departed the Xanten chapter, licking his wounds and more determined than ever to find his true path. He could scarcely know that this process would occupy the next three years of his life. Yet it would be during this crucial period that the once aimless young subdeacon managed to transform himself into the man we now recognize as Norbert of Xanten—a Gospel avatar so fanatically focused, and so mesmerizingly persuasive, that he could one day attain sainthood. If the canons back at his collegiate church would have thought such a notion preposterous, well, on that one point Norbert certainly would have agreed with them.

As Norbert withdrew from the Xanten canonry, he turned first, unsurprisingly, to his "home away from home," Siegburg

Abbey. The Benedictine community of more than a hundred monks—the leading reform institution in the Cologne archdiocese—had become a high-functioning center of literature, learning and monastic renewal, and Norbert clearly enjoyed spending time there. Still, it doesn't seem he ever gave serious consideration to throwing in with the Benedictines. In fact a different, newer foundation was now piquing his curiosity. Around this time Norbert was introduced to a community of Augustinian canons at Rolduc, west of Cologne, in what is now the Netherlands. Rolduc was only a decade old and its communal life was a radical departure from what Norbert knew at Siegburg. The Augustinians had adopted a highly austere regimen: abstaining from meat, forgoing all personal possessions and disassociating from the outside world. Norbert would become a regular visitor to Rolduc, and he took careful note of how its rule contrasted with the Benedictines, not to mention with his own secular canons at Xanten. This in turn got him contemplating which aspects of each he might cherry-pick were he starting his own community from scratch—although it's only conjecture whether, at this point, he had given such a prospect any real thought.

Rolduc figures prominently as well as the setting for another signature anecdote from the Norbert legend. In it, Norbert was saying Mass in a chapel in the abbey's dank crypt when a spider suddenly dropped from the ceiling into his chalice. As Norbert had just consecrated the wine, he felt obligated to consume it, spider and all—although in medieval times many people believed spider bites to be fatal. But later, kneeling in prayer, Norbert sneezed—and out came the spider! Grauwen and other

Norbertine historians consider this story almost certainly apocryphal, but as one of the declared miracles that fixed Norbert in the popular imagination and was cited later in support of his canonization, it bears relating. It's also a tidy illustration of the kind of colorful exploits that attached to many medieval-era saints.

Maybe Norbert's single most important influence during his reflection period was the hermit-priest Ludolf, a familiar and controversial figure to people around Xanten. Ludolf's existence was ascetic in the extreme, and he preached regularly against the evils of clerical corruption—tongue-lashings that earned him the approbation of his peasant audiences and the wrath of many clergy. Norbert spent a great deal of time with Ludolf and through him became acquainted with another reform movement, one known as "the poor of Christ," that was popular in the early twelfth century. This movement consisted of itinerant preachers—the Germans coined a word for them, *wanderpredigers*—who were committed to an almost literal emulation of the roving ministry and humble existence of Christ's own apostles. As described by the Dutch Norbertine writer A.W. van den Hurk, these roving preachers "renounced all goods and possessions, changed their monastic or canonical habits for a rough ascetic cowl of undyed wool, fed themselves with roots and herbs and slept on the bare ground. As a rule they wore rough unkempt beards, walked barefoot or traveled on a donkey while they preached peace and penance wherever they went. They had as their model St. John the Baptist and lived the Gospel to the letter."

Here was an idea that spoke powerfully to Norbert: fashioning a pared-down way of life modeled after Christ's disciples. He was so inspired, in fact, that for the next two years he dedicated himself to a quasi-hermitic existence. For his modest home he commandeered a small chapel on a hill; it was located on property his family owned in the village of Fuerstenberg, just outside Xanten. He maintained a strict daily regimen: praying, reading, scriptural study, meditation and saying Mass. Often he was fasting, and on occasion he would force himself to stay awake through the night. While these exercises were authentic expressions of penance and prayer, Norbert was also training himself in the discipline of self-mortification. And there was one more important change: like Ludolf and other eremites of his acquaintance, Norbert gradually began to step out and preach to his neighbors. Echoing his new influences, Norbert's themes too were peace, repentance, reconciliation—and, for those many clergy he maintained were leading disreputable lives, reform.

As with Ludolf, local people began to take notice. And as with Ludolf, Norbert began to collect enemies among churchmen who were feeling the sting of his criticism—a sting that, again, was especially galling given Norbert's well-known background of privilege and profligacy. One particular critic was a Benedictine theologian and writer, Rupert of Deutz, whom Norbert would have encountered at Siegburg. According to admittedly sketchy accounts, Rupert loaned Norbert a copy of one of his theological tracts, which Norbert later returned without comment. Not long after, Rupert began to hear reports of Norbert alleging that certain passages in the book were heretical. Rupert—who was said to be a prickly and argumentative type anyway—took this up with Norbert, who apparently had misunderstood his meaning. Depending on the source, Norbert may or may not have realized this, and may or may not have apologized. Either way the damage was done, and Rupert would remain an influential and lifelong critic of Norbert.

With the bad blood building up against Norbert, it was inevitable it would seek an outlet. It found one in the summer of 1118, when hundreds of high-ranking clergy from around Germany were summoned to the town of Fritzlar, east of Cologne. The main aim of the council was to again condemn Henry V, who upon the death of his nemesis Paschal had immediately set up an antipope in Rome and helped chase the newly elected Gelasius II into temporary exile. But Norbert's critics seized on this important assembly to lodge several serious charges against him. Specifically, Norbert was accused of preaching without appropriate authorization; of presenting himself as a religious when actually he belonged to no order; and of donning sheep- and goatskins to convey the impression that he was impoverished when in fact he still had considerable wealth and possessions. While these would all be considered violations of canon law, Norbert's enemies basically were accusing him of being a hypocrite. Norbert was compelled to appear at the council to explain himself.

According to his *Vitae*, he mounted a stiff defense that scarcely hid his disdain for the accusers he considered the true hypocrites. Norbertine biographer Bernard Ardura summarized Norbert's argument (with Norbert's own reported remarks in quotation):

They resent my preaching. Is it not written: "Whoever brings back a sinner from the error of his way will save his soul from death and will cover a multitude of his sins?" We have the power to preach by reason of our ordination, for the bishop said to us: "Be transmitters of the Word of God." They want to know to what religion I belong? "Religion pure and undefiled before God our Father consists in visiting orphans and widows and in keeping oneself unspotted from this world." They criticize my clothing? Does not St. Peter teach that God takes no pleasure in fine clothes? St. John the Baptist was clothed in camel's hair; St. Cecilia wore a hair shirt next to her body. Better yet, the Lord did not give our first parents a purple tunic, but garments of skin.

There was no official or clear-cut resolution to the case of this paradoxical defendant Norbert—a man well known to many of the Church leaders at Fritzlar, but as a refined noble and courtier, not the startling-looking ascetic before them now. The council leaders seem to have finessed the matter, issuing Norbert something of a rebuke but also some constructive suggestions. But on a more political level, they were beginning to appreciate that Norbert's dramatic conversion presented them with a bit of a dilemma. His passionate conviction paired with his gift for oration surely could make him a useful tool for reform; yet as an independent thinker with a stubborn streak, he might also prove hard to control. However personally motivated the charges against Norbert, and however much they wounded him—and they did—he took the chastisement to heart. It certainly would have been understandable if he had responded to Fritzlar by

rejecting Church authorities and becoming an ecclesiastic rene-
gade, as indeed many itinerant preachers were. Instead, Norbert
decided he would play by the rules. He would immediately seek
out Pope Gelasius—now in southern France—and secure his
authorization to preach. What's more, he would end any question of hypocrisy by renouncing all his worldly goods. Almost
overnight Norbert sold his property and gave the proceeds to
the poor; he gave away all his clothes; he turned over his Xanten
canonical prebend to Archbishop Frederick; and he donated his
Fuerstenberg chapel to the Siegburg Benedictines. It's even said
he gave a valuable chalice to the canons at Xanten as a sign
he bore them no ill will—and just maybe to have a satisfying
final word on their dispute. All he retained was a mule, a small
amount of money for expenses and his Mass vestments and kit.

The other lesson Norbert clearly carried away from his
"prosecution" was that he needed to leave his home area. By
now he had simply made too many enemies in Xanten and
environs; the sensitive issues he was raising, and intended to keep
raising, were hitting literally too close to home. Their fallout was
always going to be a distraction for him, or worse.

SOMETIME THAT AUTUMN, then, Norbert left behind
his little hermitage and set off. With him were two former
servants who had now apparently committed themselves to
his religious mission. They set out first for Huy, in present-day
Belgium, where Norbert abruptly decided to take his newfound

austerity one final step: He gave away the mule, and what little money he had when he left Fuerstenberg he gave to the poor. The travelers would now officially cast their lot with their fellow paupers. Despite the coming winter, Norbert was traveling in the customary fashion of a twelfth-century pilgrim—barefoot, and wearing only a woolen tunic and cloak. The three slept outdoors. They didn't beg but simply got by on whatever food they could forage and the good graces of the strangers they met.

From that point Norbert headed south, probably through the Rhone Valley, on his way to Saint-Gilles, a historic port and shipping center in Provence where Gelasius was in residence. His aim was to gain a papal audience, in order to ask forgiveness for any past transgressions (including his dual ordination, which he now recognized was arrogant, if efficient) and, more important, to secure the pope's sanction to preach. After a long journey Norbert's small band finally arrived that December. He made an impassioned case with Gelasius, detailing his lengthy discernment and why he believed God had called him to this particular ministry. Some reports have it that the pope was so taken with Norbert's obvious conviction (not to mention his high-level administrative experience) that he tried to keep him there in the papal court. But Norbert parried that invitation and left with the pope's blessing to preach anywhere in the world. In particular, Gelasius urged him to inveigh against "the many abuses and heresies" that he himself, like his messenger Norbert, believed were undermining the Church.

That charge would send Norbert back north, nearer to the monarch who continued to be Rome's most persistent tormentor. His group slogged its way amid a particularly snowy winter, Norbert preaching wherever he could find listeners. They took a more westerly route on this return trip, *wanderpredigers* by nature of their trade seldom traveling anywhere in a straight line. In Orleans, near Paris, they even managed to pick up a fourth member, a subdeacon (not named in the *Vitae*), who can be considered Norbert's first true religious disciple.

Of course, given the supposition that at this point Norbert's grasp of the French language would have been wobbly at best, his early preaching undoubtedly made for an interesting experience for cleric and congregation alike. But as to this important question of language, it should be remembered that Norbert had grown up in a busy river town not far from a region that, through history, had swung back and forth between French and German control. Given that experience, as well as his considerable diplomatic exposure in two courts, his fluency in Latin and his months-long trek to Saint-Gilles, it's likely by now he could at least make himself understood in French. Nonetheless, the *Vitae* and most historians indicate that, at this point, French remained, essentially, a foreign language to him. Even so, that little inconvenience would not have curbed his newly fired zeal to preach; Norbert would have counted on the force of his considerable personality—and just maybe the assistance of the Holy Spirit—to make himself understood. And in any case, Norbert's intention at this point was to return to the Cologne area, which would get him back to his native language and comfortably distant from his Xanten tormentors.

In March of 1119 the haggard quartet staggered into

Valenciennes, in northeast France, just in time for Norbert to be invited to celebrate Palm Sunday Mass and preach at a local church. Tragically, though, all three of Norbert's companions, no doubt suffering from the privations and exposure of their travels (and conceivably stricken with pneumonia, perhaps) now became gravely ill. Despite Norbert's ministrations, all three would die over the course of Holy Week. It was a devastating blow for Norbert, and one that left him with a profound, lingering guilt.

Meantime, it happened that the bishop of Cambrai—Norbert's associate from the imperial court, Burchard—had arranged to spend Easter in Valenciennes, which was only a short distance from his diocesan seat. Hearing this news, Norbert determined to see his friend at once. The bishop's French-speaking chaplain was somewhat taken aback at finding this weather-beaten stranger at the door, but he was eventually persuaded to convey the man inside. Norbert was emaciated and clothed virtually in rags; it was several moments before Burchard even recognized him. But once he did, the bishop's eyes welled up and he reached out to embrace his colleague. As Norbert detailed his journeys and travails, painfully recounting the loss of his associates, Burchard was greatly moved. (This was the point at which he explained to his loyal chaplain, Hugh of Fosse, that Norbert had actually declined the bishopric that he, Burchard, eventually was offered.) Then a few days later, as Norbert was about to depart Valenciennes to resume his itinerant preaching, he fell seriously ill himself. Burchard insisted Norbert stay put until he was fully recovered, and he saw to it that Norbert received constant attention. Hugh, it turns out, had been as transfixed as

Burchard by Norbert's stories from the road, and in fact the younger man had been inwardly pondering the idea of pursuing just such an apostolic ministry himself. Thus Hugh made a point of personally tending to Norbert during his convalescence, so that they might talk—as best they were able, given the language difficulties—about Norbert's plans and aspirations. (Over the course of that month it's believed Hugh also helped Norbert with his command of French.) In time Hugh committed to join Norbert, as soon as his current obligations permitted—a development that helped revive Norbert's flagging spirit.

THAT MAY, NORBERT made the short trip to Cambrai to thank Burchard. Then by June, rejoined by Hugh, he could be found preaching among the French speakers of southern Belgium, crisscrossing the villages and towns dotting the Meuse and Sambre rivers. Everywhere they went they sought out not the wealthy or titled but the commoner and the impoverished. As historian Hamish Campbell writes, "It was to those who were the most neglected spiritually, the simple uneducated country people, that Norbert went by preference and it was not long before he won their admiration and love." Everything about the pair's demeanor registered with their audiences. They sat on the ground to eat unless a person of means insisted on having them inside for a meal. Likewise, they took no money; if coins were forced on them by the well-to-do, Norbert simply turned and gave them to the poor. They had nothing beyond a mule (the animal was back as Norbert's lone concession to the mounting travel rigors), and a few prayer books for their Masses.

At this time the practice of itinerant preaching was more established in France than in Germany, where it was just beginning and had found a less hospitable audience. (That these preachers were more commonplace in France is very likely one reason why Norbert focused his initial time in French-speaking communities. Plus at this point he had the reassuring assistance of the French-speaking Hugh.) It was not hard to appreciate the appeal of the exotic, even somewhat romantic, figure of the *wanderprediger*. For peasants and serfs in the villages and countryside, there was precious little to break up the drudgery of their lives, and few ever ventured more than a couple of miles from home their entire lives. So when a traveling preacher came to town it was "an event of recreational value," writes Benjamin Mackin, "It's an event that adds color to their lives." Beyond that, at this low period in clerical history a village priest was little more than a cipher, someone who offered next to no spiritual outreach to his congregants. "He is the pawn of the feudal lord," Mackin says. "His preaching is virtually nil. He borders on the superstitious as far as liturgical activity is concerned, and hence the priest of the locale is of virtually no value to the people at all." A truly effective preacher, then, could easily step into that void and find a rapt audience—if only for an exciting day or two.

But the surging popularity of the *wanderprediger* phenomenon was also a problem for the Church. To have so many free agents roving around Europe, ostensible authority figures on scriptural meaning and Church doctrine, was dangerous. It was not much of a leap from an individual's interpretation of the Gospel to heresy. That's why the Church insisted that itinerant preachers must be licensed—to keep them under close scrutiny.

History has left us few details about precisely where Norbert traveled as an itinerant preacher. That's hardly surprising, since a man who wasn't worried about where his next meal was coming from wasn't apt to be bothered cataloguing where he'd just been. However, the *Vitae* do detail a series of remarkable events that Norbert experienced in four neighboring villages in about as many days. Since the appearances were clustered around Hugh's home of Fosse, in Belgium, and since Hugh was there with Norbert at the time, Hugh would have recalled them vividly— and no doubt considered them significant—when, decades later, the early canons of the Norbertine order were compiling Norbert's first biography. Though but a narrow window onto the duo's itinerancy, the anecdotes manage to convey the real emphasis Norbert and Hugh put on peacemaking and the reconciliation of local disputes. If that concept seems a bit alien to modern notions of Christian ministry, it should be remembered that this was a violent age when even provincial disputes were routinely bloody and not infrequently fatal. Thus, this peacemaking work from Norbert and Hugh was no small gift.

In Fosse, a crowd had gathered to hear Norbert preach. When he had concluded and was preparing to leave, Norbert and Hugh were prevailed upon to stay. The people told them about a feud between some local families that had already left dozens of people dead, and neither the local authorities nor priests could do anything to stop it. Even as they were explaining the situation to Norbert, a man came up whose brother had been one of the most recent victims. Norbert called out to him. "My dear man, I am a stranger just passing through," he said. "I have asked for nothing of anyone yet in these parts. But I would like to ask and receive that first favor from you. Grant pardon to those who killed your brother and receive your reward from God." Norbert continued to press his argument, and we are told that, in time, his message softened the man's vengeful heart and he pledged to do his part to end the killing.

Not long after, in nearby Moustier, the villagers began to gather early in the morning to see Norbert and, they hoped, a final end to this same dispute he had addressed in Fosse. Norbert, however, was locked away in a small room, deep in prayer. He remained there for so long that the crowd became restless, and after several hours they forced a reluctant Hugh to retrieve him. Norbert kept them waiting a while longer, then came out and offered a daily Mass followed by a requiem Mass for those killed in the feud. By this point the church had largely emptied. But when he finished the dual liturgies Norbert came back outside to the church courtyard, where he began to preach. And as he did, the people returned until their numbers were even larger than before. Norbert told them: "Brothers, when our Lord Jesus Christ sent his disciples out to preach, among other things he gave them the command that whatever house they entered they should first say, 'Peace be unto this house.' And if a son of peace was there, their peace would rest on him. Now we, who have become imitators of them, not by our own merits but through the superabundant grace of God, announce that same peace to you. Do not let your unbelieving minds disregard this peace because it touches on everlasting peace. You are not unaware of why we have gathered. Its accomplishment is not mine nor of my doing, since I am a stranger and a traveler, but it is of the will and power of God. It is for you, however, to comply with his will with complete and total affection."

When Norbert finished preaching, the *Vitae* say, people on both sides of the dispute began to talk over what they had heard, then gathered their church's precious relics around them and in prayerful communion agreed to settle their conflict.

The next day, we learn, Norbert went to yet another village, Gembloux. His reputation now racing ahead of him, Norbert found another crowd already waiting. They were hopeful he might reconcile two local lords whose feuding had devastated the village. Norbert sought out one of the antagonists and told him, in effect, that while the man was certainly powerful, his power derived solely from God—whose humble messenger Norbert was. "Receive the commands of the Lord your God," Norbert admonished him. "Forgive the one who has offended you so that you may be forgiven and thus the consolation of the poor and needy might bring about the remission of your sins." Touched both by Norbert's humility and his message, this lord said he would entertain a settlement. Norbert then found the second lord and again began to make the case for peace. Unlike his opponent, this second man spewed invective at Norbert until there was no point in continuing. Returning to the first noble-man, Norbert declared, "The man is mad, but he will soon fall and be captured and be trampled down by his enemies." And within the week, we are told, that is precisely what happened.

The last of these connected visits from the *Vitae* occurred in Corroy. The villagers filled their church for Norbert's Mass, after which he inquired whether they were experiencing any serious disputes. People mentioned several antagonists by name—one of whom, a soldier, was there among them. Hearing his name called, he darted outside and mounted his horse to leave. But when he spurred the animal, it didn't move. No matter how hard the soldier jabbed at it, the horse refused to budge. The crowd, having followed him outside and witnessing this, began to laugh and to mock him; some declared it a sign from God. Shaken, the soldier dismounted, went back into the church, prostrated himself and asked forgiveness.

Even allowing for the *Vitae*'s hagiographic gloss, it is clear the peacemaking motif was a major one throughout the wanderings of Norbert and Hugh. So it went with these two, through that summer and fall, in village after village after village. It's not hard to imagine what a scene they must have made: this gaunt, dirty and unkempt man, barefoot and wearing the plain wool tunic of a pauper, like a prophet who had walked right out of the Old Testament, accompanied by his eager young associate still dressed in canonical black. One can almost see Norbert rising before the assembled villagers, their initial curiosity turning to amazement as they hear him, with his combination of conviction and compassion, and then graduating to astonishment when he speaks of things actually apropos of their own humble lives. More than that, here was a priest (or so he said) who even invited their questions! This man Norbert was entertaining and genuine and charismatic, and by all accounts the people embraced him.

As best as we can tell from the meager historical record, this year of 1119 maybe marked Norbert's only true period as a *wanderprediger*. Circumstances were about to conspire again to send Norbert's life and mission in a different direction. But it was time enough to reinforce the sense that itinerant preaching was perhaps his true passion and gift, and in fact the rest of his life he would never really stop traveling and preaching. Mackin points out the irony that one of the abiding principles of the Norbertine order, from very early days, was that you stayed and worked where you took your vows. Norbert himself, however, is "very much a man who is the antithesis of what later in the history of the order was subsumed under the rubric of 'stability in place,' or *stabilitas in loco*," Mackin writes. "He's a very foot-loose man. He never settled down. If anything, it's a wonder... that a [Norbertine] community was ever formed at all."

Indeed, after Norbert established his order at Prémontré, he would leave the community whenever he could to go back on the road. And even as the exalted archbishop of Magdeburg, he mounted the pulpit every chance he got. The Church would forever keep pushing Norbert into the leadership precincts of its various organizations; he was forever pushing back to commune with the common people. He couldn't help himself. "From 1118 onward, Norbert is and remains a pilgrim," observes Grauwen, "a displaced person, expelled from his country, wandering about because of the Kingdom of God."

CHAPTER 5

THE PREMONSTRATENSIAN

As it happened, just one month after having sanctioned Norbert's preaching, Pope Gelasius took ill and died. A new pontiff, Callixtus II—another strong reform figure—was elected, and he immediately called for another general council of Church hierarchy. It would be held in Reims, in the northeast of France, that October. Since Norbert was still preaching in the region, that proved convenient as he believed the election of a new pope required him to renew his authorization. So that autumn he and Hugh of Fosse, accompanied by another acolyte, made their way to Reims. Once there, Norbert found himself preaching in front of audiences that sometimes included more politically connected and educated listeners than he had met with out in the countryside. In this way he broadened his reputation for a bold message and uniquely charismatic style. Nonetheless, his sole aim in Reims was to secure an audience with Callixtus.

With hundreds of Church officials on the scene and an important council for a new pope to manage, Callixtus was rather too preoccupied to meet with itinerant ascetics. So despite Norbert's best efforts he was unable to arrange an encounter. After several days he left Reims, despondent. Having gone to such lengths to legitimize his preaching, Norbert wasn't sure what he would do if that was again called into question.

A few miles outside Reims, the little group took a rest by the side of the road. Soon there appeared a large group of lords and clerics, the retinue of an important bishop arriving for the council. The bishop stopped and made time to inquire after Norbert, who in turn explained his dilemma and his need to obtain an audience with the pope. The bishop responded that he could probably arrange that, and that if Norbert's group came back to Reims with him he would try.

This was Bartholomew of Laon, France—an influential churchman of his period. Not only did he oversee one of the most strategic cities in the empire and a center of Church reform and intellectual activity, but he was also a nephew of Callixtus. (The king of France was another relative.) Bartholomew had become bishop of Laon in 1113, and in the most dire of circumstances—a violent popular revolt against a reviled predecessor had left that bishop dead and the cathedral, and many other of Laon's churches, in ashes. But in the relatively short time since his installation, the able Bartholomew was already rebuilding the cathedral and was now putting the same vigor into the spiritual renewal of the entire diocese.

Thrilled by this turn of events, Norbert returned to the general council, where the bishop did manage to introduce the ragged *wanderprediger* to his uncle Callixtus. Because the heavy council schedule would not really permit a discussion of any consequence, the pope told Bartholomew and Norbert that he would come to Laon afterward—it was not far from Reims—

and they could pick up the matter there.

In most Norbert retellings, dating back to Herman of Tournai, the meeting with Bartholomew by the side of the road is cast as something that happened entirely by chance, and perhaps it was. As that meeting would turn out to be so consequential for Norbert's life and legacy, it's easy to appreciate why supporters would have wanted to memorialize it like something ordained by providence. On the other hand, it's fair to wonder if the encounter was actually so serendipitous. Bartholomew came from Laon, where Norbert had family from his mother's side; given their noble lineage they would surely have been known to the bishop. If so, and imagining the family's concern for Norbert's shaky health, it wouldn't be surprising if someone alerted Bartholomew to look for him at Reims. Then there's the fact that this council was occurring just one year after the controversy at Fritzlar, and so Bartholomew might well have been aware of Norbert from that event, too. There's no way to know what really happened with certainty, but clearly God wasn't the only one looking out for his humble servant Norbert at Reims. And either way, it's hard to dispute what Benjamin Mackin observes about the role of the bishop of Laon in Norbertine history. "The fact is," he writes, "there wouldn't have been any community at Prémontré had not…Bartholomew intervened and put pressure on [Norbert] to settle down and to take the group that had formed around him to [establish] a definite community at Prémontré."

After the Reims council, Callixtus stayed with Bartholomew in Laon for several days, giving pope, preacher and bishop ample time to discuss Norbert's situation—and affording the two prelates a much better sense of this ragged *wanderprediger* with the nobleman's pedigree. Did the pope in fact renew Norbert's permission to continue preaching? Probably, and that is the assumption of most Norbertine histories, though there is no clear-cut proof other than the fact that Norbert would eventually preach again. More recently, some scholars have suggested that Callixtus might actually have withheld his approval—not to punish Norbert but out of genuine concern for his well-being. Anyone spending even a short amount of time with Norbert would have immediately grasped the toll exacted on his health by the constant travel and impoverished circumstances. Beyond that, Callixtus and Bartholomew almost certainly wished to channel Norbert's obvious talents, by which they would have had in mind some fitting assignment within the formal Church structure—and something where authorities could at least keep an eye on him, if not a leash.

Given his concern, Callixtus directed that Norbert be put under Bartholomew's personal care, and the bishop's first order of business was to keep his itinerant new friend there in Laon for a while. For once, that didn't prove to be difficult. Winter was coming on, and with Hugh needing to return to Cambrai to finish up some personal and clerical obligations, Norbert was amenable to staying in Laon and regaining his strength. It would also give him the opportunity to see his family there. So it was that Norbert spent the winter of 1119–20 in Laon. The additional appeal of a three- or four-month hiatus was that he could take advantage of Laon's renowned cathedral school, which drew scholar-instructors and brilliant young men from all over the continent. Though we're not sure, many believe Norbert in fact used the opportunity to delve more deeply into the Psalms, attend lectures on philosophy and continue to polish his French.

Bartholomew and Callixtus weighed various options for keeping Norbert in Laon. What they eventually settled on was pressing him to accept the position of superior over a small group of canons at a Laon church. This community of canons, located at St. Martin's, was notoriously lackadaisical as to its spiritual obligations and had no real interest in living by a formal rule; indeed, for several decades it had stubbornly resisted efforts at reform. But reform is precisely what Bartholomew wished Norbert to undertake.

Norbert was conflicted about this, at best. He knew this was an extraordinary opportunity, he liked Laon well enough, and he had grown quite close to Bartholomew. On the other hand, he was anxious to resume his preaching regimen. And, no doubt still smarting from his failure with the canons at Xanten, he was certainly aware of a Church truism: it is far easier to form a new religious community than reform an existing one that has lost its way. So with great deference, he reminded the pope that the reason he had worked so hard to transform his life, and why he had given away all his earthly goods, was in order to preach to the people and lead the apostolic life. Ultimately, Norbert said, he would of course do whatever the pope desired of him—but in this case, he stipulated, only if the St. Martin's community agreed to live on his terms. And those terms, as described by A.W. van den Hurk, were daunting: "This meant to be voluntarily poor, to renounce the world, to accept and carry scorn and

revilement, injustice, insult, hunger, thirst and other hardships."
This would come to be known as Norbert's *propositum*—his goal,
his purpose, his life ideal. And it must be said it was also a clever
gambit, for Norbert surely knew what would happen next. When
the St. Martin's canons began to get the picture of the harsh
life Norbert had in store for them, they rejected his "offer" in no
uncertain terms. And Norbert was off the hook—for the moment.

It's not difficult to imagine Bartholomew's frustration at this
point. With spring just around the corner—and with its arrival
Norbert's departure—there was perhaps a touch of desperation
in the bishop's voice when he offered up one more possibility
for his picky ward: Well, if not St. Martin's, why don't you form
your *own* community?

EVEN TODAY, WHEN YOU travel to Prémontré you are
struck by how remote it is. Approach it from any direction and
you will descend twisty, narrow roads through a thick primeval
forest right out of a fairy tale. Here and there, neat stacks of
huge, freshly hewn trees attest that timbering remains important
to the region, as it has done for centuries.

The progressive Bartholomew, as part of his reform-
renewal agenda, was known for encouraging new monasteries
from a variety of orders. In raising this new possibility, the
bishop also reminded Norbert of something he had often
said—that he believed God meant for him to live in a remote
and solitary location (and Bartholomew certainly had plenty of

those scattered around his diocese). Norbert acknowledged that point, but he added that he would only undertake to found a community if he could attract associates who were willing to follow him in this vision. And that stark vision was essentially the one he had sketched out for the canons of St. Martin—with the additional hardship of being distanced from civilization.

Still, Norbert's proviso was enough to encourage Bartholomew. The bishop began to escort Norbert to prospective locations he hoped might be sufficiently isolated for his friend's purposes. Alas, none of the initial sites he showed him passed muster. Then one day Bartholomew hit on the idea of taking him to a spot in an ancient forest, located about ten miles west of Laon. As they descended on horseback farther and farther into a valley, the woods closed in on them from all sides. Finally they arrived at their destination, a small clearing; the only thing standing was a little chapel dedicated to St. John the Baptist. Another religious community had built it some years back before abandoning the site, finding it basically uninhabitable. A scattered handful of hermits remained in the area, but that was about the extent of the humanity in beautiful—but apparently God-forsaken—Prémontré.

After they surveyed the surroundings, Norbert and Bartholomew spent time in prayer at the chapel. As the afternoon wore on, the bishop suggested they had better start heading back before it got too dark. But Norbert surprised his host and asked that he be allowed to stay at the chapel overnight, in further prayer and contemplation. Bartholomew warily agreed—although he was concerned enough for Norbert that he had his men return with some food and provisions.

When Bartholomew came back the next morning he asked Norbert what he wished to do. But he could already see that his friend was elated; Prémontré, it seems, was the place. According to the account of Herman of Tournai, Norbert said, "I will remain here, Father, because I know that God has destined this place for me. This will be a place of rest for me, and here many will be saved by the grace of God." Overnight Norbert had experienced what he considered a divine revelation, and he shared with Bartholomew the clear visions he'd had of men in procession wearing white robes, all carrying silver crosses and incense-laden censers and lighted candles. (As for its name, this secluded opening in the forest had always been known as Prémontré, it seems. The name is thought to derive from the Latin *pratum monstratum*—meaning a clearing or meadow that is "pointed out." The Norbertines have always considered this particularly apt since Prémontré seems to have been "pointed out" to Norbert by God.)

With this turn Bartholomew was elated too, and he set about the complicated arrangements to transfer the Prémontré property to Norbert. Of course, it's easy to appreciate why Bartholomew was so enthusiastic by the development. Maybe the bigger mystery is why Norbert—"the fervent preacher he was, and remained," in the words of Wilfried Grauwen—was all of a sudden willing to settle down and establish a monastery. Grauwen does point out that at this time, it was not unusual for *wanderpredigers* to eventually gather their followers into formal communities. And as we have seen, Norbert had been studying various religious communities for years and had clearly given thought to what a "Norbertine" institution would look like, if the opportunity ever presented itself. Perhaps he simply decided that opportunity was now and that this new place, Prémontré, was in fact the "remote and solitary" home of his longtime intuition. The only thing we know for sure is that once Norbert made the decision to pursue his own community, he did so with his customary unbridled zeal.

Divine revelation aside, the remoteness of the foundational Premonstratensian site is such that, even nine hundred years later, you sense that Norbert must have been rather intentional in choosing it. He surely understood that if a disciple was to follow him there—a place truly in the middle of nowhere, its thick forests dotted with bogs and swamps where the only company might be the wolves, wild boars, bears and other predators that abounded there—well, this is someone who is *serious* about his vocation. Certainly there would be little of the secular world to tempt Norbert's recruits! Then again, for all its apparent isolation, Prémontré did make some strategic sense as well. As Hamish Campbell points out, Prémontré, though seemingly off the beaten track, was situated near the intersection of two traditional European travel routes—one from England to Italy (via Calais and Basel, on the Rhine in present-day Switzerland) and the other from Germany (through Cologne and Paris) to the Mediterranean. Laon was a major hub of Church reform, yet it was also near Norbert's German homeland as well as his family and political connections. Bartholomew was an enthusiastic— not to mention well-connected and generous—champion. And

finally, Campbell writes, "It was near one of the great intellectual centers of the day, the cathedral school of Laon, which was to
give several of its best men to Prémontré."

That last point was crucial, for Norbert had taken title, for
now, to a religious community with no people in it. His new
order was still an idea, and it would remain just that unless or
until others followed him there.

Thus in the early spring of 1120 Norbert returned to the
road, but this time his preaching would have a more self-inter-
ested motive: Could he convince enough people to come lead a
communal life based on the prayerful, humble, Gospel-witness-
ing example of Christ's apostles? Would they be willing to give
over their personal possessions for the larger good of the community? Would they be able to understand, much less endure,
the physical and emotional hardships waiting for them in a place
they had never seen? Norbert was about to find out.

He went first to familiar territory, to Cambrai. Hugh was
still tending to his affairs (he would join Norbert at Prémontré
later on) but Norbert began to preach about his new vision. And
his first recruit turned out to be one of the most important. A
young, Belgian-born cleric named Evermode was so enamored
of Norbert that he signed up on the spot. And in fact Evermode would remain with Norbert, in every sense—on the rest
of this recruiting trip, as one of his most able lieutenants in the
order's formative years, as a bishop, as founder of a number of
Norbertine communities. And Evermode, like Norbert, would
eventually be venerated as a saint.

From there the two men returned to various Belgian communities in the region where, just a year earlier, Norbert had made such a name in settling local disputes. In Nivelles, they were joined by a man named Anthony, who was also destined to be a prominent early Norbertine figure. The three continued on to Laon, where at the cathedral school Norbert managed to secure the commitments of seven of the best students there, all of them from affluent Lorraine families. This cohort was so remarkable that all seven were destined to be bishops and abbots—among them Anselm of Havelberg, who would go on to become a celebrated bishop, critic, writer and diplomat.

So it went over that frantic first month or so that, by Easter Sunday of 1120, there were fourteen men at Prémontré—Norbert and thirteen intrepid disciples. Bartholomew himself came to Prémontré to oversee the sacred liturgy and distribute to all the white habit that has ever since been the Norbertines' signature. There would be a community after all.

IN THOSE EARLIEST DAYS of the community, Norbert's followers busied themselves erecting crude huts, very likely surrounding the small St. John the Baptist chapel, which was literally at the center of all their activities. Norbert oversaw the observation of the daily office, but when the community was not in prayer its focus was almost exclusively on work—hard manual labor. There were fields to clear, crops to plant and cultivate, water to draw and haul, animals to be tended (and their stables built and cleaned). There is speculation the men would have erected some kind of guest house, since that was a customary and expected monastic feature. An overgrown orchard planted by the earlier settlement needed to be reclaimed. One of the earliest priorities seems to have been the development of fish ponds, and eventually there would be seven of these as part of a site totaling more than sixty acres.

It was gritty, grimy work, and in consideration of that—and in a manifestation of the austere life they had chosen—the men during their labor wore not the white habits but the rough wool tunics of the peasant. Through that first spring and summer the community continued to attract some new members, and it's also likely that Bartholomew put the eremites who lived around Prémontré under Norbert's protection. Among other things, that meant they quickly outgrew their little chapel, and Norbert began making arrangements with stonemasons throughout the region about construction of a bigger, more permanent one.

In fact, Norbert was overseeing everything. At this point he was not so much the father-superior as a father figure. In truth, he had gathered about him what was basically a cult of personality that he now needed to mold into a true religious community. These were (mostly) young men who had much more passion than experience, more enthusiasm than knowledge. Norbert preached to them every morning and every evening. As was the case when he addressed lay audiences, he spoke simply but eloquently, eschewing an Olympian style for a more accessible one. And his message "was both theoretical and practical," says Grauwen. "Like an eagle teaching its fledglings to fly, he in fact showed them by his example how the religious life they had

chosen should be." He was constantly teaching, patiently school-
ing his followers in the discipline and practices of conventional
monasteries. And he was constantly encouraging, bucking up
his proteges as they went about their often back-breaking labors.

Indeed, Norbert himself was still sorting out what formal rule
he would adopt for this new community. It was already decided
and understood by everyone who had come to Prémontré that
they were to be canons regular—which is to say, their primary
commitment would be to their priestly ministry, yet they would
live in community. But as canons, Norbert knew they definitely
needed to follow a formal rule.

Month by month, project by project, their first year passed—
but not without the occasional setback. Some of the recruits left
when the labor and privation overwhelmed any initial romantic notions they may have come with. And it is said that one
of those who absconded apparently took with him the money
that Norbert's Laon followers had entrusted to him when they
agreed to divest their personal holdings. This of course put even
more hardship on the wilderness homesteaders, but Norbert—
who since his conversion was always wary of having any money
in his pocket—took it as a sign that they were intended to live
through their wits, and God's grace.

Eventually Norbert needed to turn his full attention to the
new church. At this time, it was customary for any church of
consequence to acquire saintly relics, and in the middle of 1121
he set himself to that task. The wealthy archdiocese of Cologne
was known to possess large quantities of relics, and Norbert
used his connections to arrange something of a shopping trip.

Sometime that summer or early autumn, and now reunited with Hugh, he traveled to Cologne. There they were able to acquire remains of St. Ursula and some companions who had been martyred in the fourth century. Soon after, according to the order's tradition, Norbert was authorized as well to take some relics of St. Gereon, whose remains were believed to be buried beneath the church named for him. The problem was, no one really knew where. With a number of abbots and monks there with him, all praying for inspiration in this sober undertaking, Norbert suddenly directed the work crew to unearth one particular spot. The assembly of prelates expressed great surprise at this, since to their knowledge that site had never been associated with a burial. And yet when the workers dug, there was Gereon!

Coming back by way of Namur, in present-day Belgium, Norbert's group met a countess who, having heard many tales of Norbert and been made aware that he was now passing through, arranged to intercept him. She and her husband owned a number of churches in the region, she told Norbert, and they wished to see the largest of these converted into a monastery. (Later scholarship suggests Norbert was a useful vehicle at that particular moment, as the noble couple were feuding with their local bishop.) In any case, she prevailed on Norbert to undertake this mission, and Norbert agreed. The count and countess deeded the several churches to Norbert and gave him a generous endowment, as well as cultivated lands, vineyards, forests and other resources to create and manage the new monastery. For his part, Norbert left behind some of his newly acquired relics, and he vowed to send back some of his followers to establish the monastery.

This was in November of 1121. It was a stunning and bold development, especially considering that Prémontré was still in its infancy. "The first foundation had not received a fixed organization," notes Grauwen. "His followers had not yet made their religious profession and no rule had been chosen. And yet Norbert accepts a second foundation far from the diocese of Laon, situated at a great distance from the first one, with a completely different endowment and in completely different surroundings... ." It offers further proof as well of the alacrity, even rashness, with which Norbert often moved when given the chance—or as Grauwen puts it, the idea that "once Norbert has taken the right direction he rushes on full speed." Indeed, just like that, the Church of Our Lady of Floreffe became the second Norbertine institution.

Norbert scurried back to Prémontré for what would be a busy Advent season. By that Christmas, some forty men—mostly clerics but also some lay brothers—constituted the emerging community. At a candlelit midnight Mass, all forty made their formal profession to Norbert's order and put themselves in the service of the Church of Prémontré. One by one they read aloud a document detailing that commitment, signed it, and then placed it on the altar. Each agreed to live according to the Rule of St. Augustine, as it had come to be interpreted by Norbert. As the solemn night gave way to Christmas morning, the tired members of the Catholic Church's newest religious community no doubt looked around and took inspiration from what they had been able to build, virtually from nothing.

They were the first Premonstratensians.

CHAPTER 6

THE GARDENER

At this evolutionary moment in Church history there were basically two kinds of religious orders: monks, who led highly regimented lives of contemplation, prayer and manual labor and had virtually no interaction with the outside world; and canons, who also lived in community but, being priests and deacons (not all monks were ordained), had a variety of liturgical and professional responsibilities to others. In the monastic world it was self-evident that communities needed some kind of formal guideline, or "rule"—such as that laid down in the sixth century by St. Benedict—to live by. A rule ensured there was consistency from foundation to foundation as to the monks' mission, priorities and daily routine. But as to which religious orders followed the "right" kind of rule, or the most effective, or the most devout—well, on these political points there remained considerable disagreement. Rivalries and sibling jealousies between different orders were common, and criticisms freely offered, if not always appreciated.

Where canons were concerned, however, it was an open question as to whether a formal rule was essential. As we have seen, in communities of so-called secular canons—those clerical groups attached to a specific church as opposed to a religious order—the Church had tried hard to impose reform regimens, largely borrowed from the more contemplative communities. The stubborn resistance that met those efforts was an indication of the general distaste many canons had for the monastic way of life. This was understandable enough; if canons had wanted to take vows of poverty and spend their lives in reflective silence, they would have opted for cloisters rather than canonries in the first place.

Certainly in the very early days at Prémontré, where the principals and the key early disciples were all canons, it was hardly a given that a formal rule was necessary. In that embryonic phase, of course, the Premonstratensians tended to simply look to their leader, and Norbert told them what to do and why. For most that arrangement seemed quite satisfactory. But Norbert and his second-in-command, Hugh of Fosse, knew better. Prémontré was *not* a secular canonry; it was a religious community whose members happened to be canons. Unlike their young acolytes, Norbert and Hugh understood that without the discipline of a rule their fledgling community might well struggle after its initial surge of adrenalin wore off. Besides, now that a second foundation had already been added, at Floreffe, it would be essential to set down clear markers as to principles and common practices. And whether the founder realized it at the time, Floreffe was only the beginning of what would soon be a rapidly expanding Norbertine world.

Having undertaken Prémontré, Norbert had inquired of many Catholic prelates and thinkers as to what kind of rule he should adopt. Because of the uniqueness of the community there were various options available to him, and he got back various opinions. But in truth Norbert had come to the experiment with a strong preference already in mind. All along his overriding purpose in establishing Prémontré was to create an environment where even priests who worked in the wider world could aspire to the "apostolic life"—and could lead that life even in community, even in one place. So his intent was to adopt a rule that best facilitated that ideal. It was no surprise, then, when Norbert reached back for this need to the venerable Augustine, bishop of Hippo. Centuries before, Augustine had created a rule for priests who lived together but also served others—canons. Now, during the age of Gregorian reform, Augustine's ideal of the apostolic life had been rediscovered and revived. The more rigorous communities of canons regular (the *ordo novus*) followed the earliest iteration of Augustinian rule, known as the *ordo monasterii*, which was rather succinct and dealt primarily with how a community's prayers and singing of psalms were to be conducted throughout the day and at different seasons of the year. Norbert initially adopted this form of the rule at Prémontré; like some other reformers, however, he came to consider the *ordo monasterii* outdated and insufficient to his needs. So he soon replaced it with the *Praeceptum*, a later and much fuller guide to community life from Augustine that is now widely considered his "Rule."

With these Augustinian precepts as his foundation, Norbert ultimately established for his followers a rigid way of life similar to the one he had witnessed in the Rolduc community. But in

Norbert's application, it was even more austere. Everyday life at Prémontré was, in general, one of absolute silence, routine privation and great regimentation—to the point that an outside observer at the time could be forgiven if he mistook the first Norbertine community for a Benedictine or Cistercian monastery. When Norbert's followers were accepted into the community, their resources went into the community, too. But in those early days Prémontré needed outside help as well, especially the generous patronage of Bartholomew, and so one of Norbert's first major goals was to reach the point, and as soon as possible, where the community could survive entirely on its own means and labors. The Premonstratensian day was punctuated by the Liturgy of the Hours—the community rising at midnight and again at dawn to pray, then coming together at other assigned times until Compline was said just before bedtime. Between these times of common prayer there were the endless chores, the building and the clearing and the cultivating, but Norbert set aside ample time as well for contemplation and theological study, especially for his clergy.

While in those first days there was no real "parish work" in such an isolated location, Norbert was preparing his priests for the ministerial work he was confident would come, and there was intensive training for those deacons and subdeacons who were still working toward their priestly ordinations. Initially the community made do with only one meal a day, at midafternoon.

Then there was the signature Premonstratensian "look." Unlike canons most anywhere else, who wore black robes, the members of the Prémontré community wore white—Norbert's attention-getting testament to the purity of Premonstratensian devotion, and in particular to the mystery of the Resurrection, which had a special place in the new order's spiritual life. So it was that the Norbertines were soon known in Church circles as the "White Canons" or "White Fathers," and remain so to this day.

Central to all else at Prémontré was liturgical prayer—which, after all, was the heart of the canonical life—and Norbert personally set a particular emphasis on celebration of the Eucharist. This sacrament, while always the centerpiece of the Mass, was taking on an even more conspicuous importance in the medieval Church, and Norbert was so thoroughly committed to this movement that in time his name would become almost synonymous with the Eucharist. In fact, beyond the regular expectations of his Augustinian regimen, Norbert constantly reinforced several of his own core values with the community, and the first of these pertained to the Eucharist. To give appropriate glory to God and out of respect for the Eucharistic celebration at the core of the Catholic faith, Norbert insisted that his churches—and the altar in particular—should be beautifully adorned and always kept as clean as possible. Indeed, their daily liturgy was virtually the only time the Premonstratensians exchanged their rough and soiled work robes for immaculate linen vestments.

Equally important to Norbert was the correction of faults. It stands to reason that a reformer wasn't timid about pointing out another's shortcomings, and while Norbert presumably learned to do this with more tact as he got older, it never stopped being a priority for him. This was especially true in the earliest days of

Prémontré, with Norbert aware that the community's very existence could rise or fall on the discipline established at the start. "He knew that without a constant effort at self-improvement slackness creeps in and eventually infects the whole community," says Hamish Campbell. Put another way, Norbert's criticisms were not meant to carp at or embarrass an individual but to help his community attain a higher, and purer, devotion to God.

Norbert's third core value was to be hospitable always—an idea transcending simple kindness or courtesy, one speaking to the Gospel injunction that you will love your neighbor, feed him when he is hungry, shelter him when he is weary or homeless, and care for him when he is sick. Norbert considered these admonitions basic to the apostolic life, and as an itinerant preacher he had been the recipient of such gestures countless times from others.

As is evident, this "Norbertine" way was a demanding one, an eclectic amalgamation of Norbert's own ascetic experiences and his lofty expectations of others. The combination of this approach's uniqueness and harshness also made it a hard thing to put across in a new community—especially one that was not technically monastic. For all their devotion to Norbert, some followers questioned whether his interpretation of Augustine was even authentic—or, related, why it had to be so severe. At such times Norbert would gently but firmly reassure them, saying that "all the ways of the Lord are mercy and truth" and that the details of their rule mattered less than their dedication to it. Says the Norbertine writer Dino suor Santa, "Even if different, they are not contrary. Even if institutions and customs vary, the bond of charity remains the same. First God must be loved, then the neighbor."

IN HIS APPROACH TO a rule for Prémontré, as with all else in his life, Norbert was true to his nonconformist self. What others might think of his actions mattered less to him than whether they comported with God's plan for him. He adapted a rule that, whatever its technical source, best suited both his personal theology and the realities of managing a viable community in the middle of the wilderness. Though ascetic, he was also pragmatic. Almost as soon as Prémontré got under way, Norbert began altering some of his more extreme rules just to get things done. The community loosened its fasting regimen, for instance, because there simply was too much work to be done on such a meager intake of fuel. As for the code of absolute silence—well, it's hard for a work crew to erect a building when people can't talk to one another. So the community arranged for designated places and times when necessary conversation could occur.

Nevertheless, the Prémontré experiment came in for an inordinate amount of criticism from other Church voices. Norbert was taken to task for not following the "legitimate" Augustinian rule (the *ordo monasterii*), or for corrupting it, or for taking liberties with the Catholic liturgy, or for other supposed offenses. As had been true when Norbert was criticized at Fritzlar, this opposition tended to be couched in canonical technicalities but was really meant as a broader rebuke of the man himself. As indicated earlier, much of this carping was of a piece with this turbulent period in Church history, the great "sorting out" in which factions parsed which reforms were legitimate and which went too far and leaned into heresy. But a good bit of it sprang from what many considered a certain effrontery and presumptuousness from a spiritual upstart. For now, and for the rest of his life, the bold iconoclast Norbert would be regarded with both great admiration and great suspicion.

For his part, Norbert—who still had his powerful protectors, it must be remembered—tried to avoid these political traps as best he could and keep the larger view in mind. And, truth be told, the believers were voting with their feet. Despite the austerity Norbert had on offer, there was a tremendous popular appeal in what was happening at Prémontré. At this moment in history the apostolic movement was spreading like a fire in the wilderness, an idea that spoke to both the peasant classes (who understood in their bones that Christ and his apostles had been speaking directly to their plight) and to nobles who had grown weary of the endless warring between monarchs and popes and themselves yearned for a Gospel-inspired goodness in their lives. These impulses were reinforced by the initial high-mindedness of the first Crusades, the Gregorian reform movement in the Church, and even the apocalyptic fervor that then gripped much of Christianity. Taken together, it meant that people of all walks were contemplating the spiritual dimension of their lives. And in almost no time so many of them were streaming into the woods of Prémontré that Norbert and Hugh could hardly keep up.

Indeed, one of the main ways Norbert was a reformer

was in reimagining who could be in a religious community. "All manner of people—men, women and children—came to Prémontré and simply took up residence there to be around this spiritual leader, this person who suddenly introduces into the life of the people of that area a sense of the divine, a sense of the spiritual, a sense of Christ," writes Benjamin Mackin. At Prémontré there quickly developed three related but distinct subcommunities. First were the clerics. Within a few years of its settlement there were said to be some eighty priests, deacons and subdeacons at the site. Another group was lay men, who quickly numbered many hundreds. Some of these were educated or highborn, but most were illiterate peasants or artisans who shouldered the bulk of the manual labor in the community. These workmen might have attended liturgies and some of the daily offices as they were able, but in general they did the same kinds of jobs in building Prémontré that they would have been doing for their lords on an estate: farming, timbering, milling, carpentry, tending to animals.

Then there were the women. Prémontré was a "double monastery," meaning that it was a single religious entity that included both men *and* women. Double monasteries were known to exist here and there in the first millennium of the Church, but they had essentially disappeared by the tenth century. However, like so many other spiritual traditions, such paired houses were now seeing a resurgence. This was also due to the fact that the most effective itinerant preachers, like Norbert, were as inspirational to women as to men, and so their religious communities drew vocations among both sexes.

It's not absolutely clear when women appeared at Prémon-tré, but we know it was almost from the beginning. The first woman on record there would also be one of its most histor-ically prominent. Her name was Ricvera, and she was a wid-owed French noblewoman who gave up all her possessions to join Norbert's community, and who quickly assumed leadership of the growing company of women there. Thanks to some accounts from Herman of Tournai (as opposed to the *Vitae* of Norbert, which are curiously silent on the women of Prémon-tré), we have a solid sense of what life was like for Ricvera and her sisters in those early years. In short, their routine seems to have been even more austere than that of the men. Most stayed within the physical confines of their house. Their hair was shorn unappealingly short. They wore simple wool or sheepskin robes. They exchanged their silk or lace veils for cheap black head-cloths. They abstained from meat and were often fasting beyond the normal obligations of the Church calendar. They followed the daily office, and when not in prayer they were expected to sew, cook, bake bread, spin thread and do other household tasks in support of the larger community. Constant silence was of course the rule, and it was rigidly enforced. "They may speak to no man," writes Theodore Antry, "not even a brother or rela-tive, except at the window in the church and then only with two lay brothers with the man on the outside and two women who reside with her on the inside. They hear everything that is said."

It was typical of double monasteries that men and women were segregated into two distinct houses, each connected to the church but on opposite sides, and that was probably the case at

Prémontré. In addition to the routine chores expected of them, the women, under Ricvera's direction, operated the community's hostel. This had been built to accommodate travelers but also functioned as a place where the poor could come for food and shelter, and as a rudimentary hospital for the sick. Many of the women at Prémontré had pledged deep, lifelong commitments to the religious life. But "lay sisters" were welcome at Prémontré too. They did not have to turn over their possessions and their vows of poverty and chastity were temporary; they could return home if and when they wished.

The double monastery at Prémontré teemed in those earliest decades; within a few years of its founding it is thought that the women there numbered more than a thousand. This popularity owed not only to Norbert's immense appeal and the apostolic movement generally, but to the fact that some orders didn't accept women. Most of the other early Norbertine foundations were established as double monasteries, while some locations built affiliated convents nearby. But this close coexistence of Norbertine men and women would not last for long. About a decade after Norbert's death, in a general chapter under Hugh's direction, the Norbertines decided to follow the lead of most other religious orders and cease the construction and operation of double monasteries. Was this a reaction to specific problems with the coexistence of sexes? Or a more profound philosophical objection? We don't know; the record doesn't really explain it. We only know that, henceforth, Norbertine canonesses and lay sisters would be in their own dedicated foundations. Not having priests immediately at hand for their liturgical and sacramental purposes made it extremely challenging for such communities to sustain their monastic ideal, and so the involvement of women religious in the Premonstratensian order declined dramatically until, a few centuries on, it became practically nonexistent. Still, some Norbertine women's communities did persist, and even today there are a number of them within the order (including a priory of some forty nuns that was recently founded near Tehachapi, California).

WHEN HE ESTABLISHED Prémontré, Norbert might occasionally permit himself the satisfaction of thinking he was sparking a new movement—but chances are he *didn't* dwell much on the countless and tedious details of day-to-day management. For him the community was more a freshly planted garden that required constant tending, and one that needed to grow. That meant Norbert still needed to travel, making additional converts for the Lord and in the process additional recruits for himself. Besides, it had never been Norbert's intention to let the establishment of a religious community divert him entirely from his preaching apostolate. If he could no longer be a full-time *wanderprediger*, it was still his plan that once his new community got its adolescent legs, and once seasonal weather returned, he would be back on the road.

He could do that because he had a number of extraordinary people he could lean on, none more so than the trusty Hugh of Fosse. Some fifteen to twenty years younger than Norbert, Hugh

was devoted to his superior and utterly shared his passion for
the apostolic life. Everyone who knew them appreciated what
extraordinarily divergent and yet complementary figures these
two were: the mentor and the student; the quintessential idea
man and the brilliant detail man; the one who came alive in
front of an audience and the one who was almost painfully shy;
the one whose head was usually in the heavens and the one who
kept his eyes squarely on earth. Norbert made Hugh the first
superior of Prémontré, and he "was generally looked upon as
the older brother in this large family that grew daily with new
arrivals, converted by the words of Norbert," writes Bernard
Ardura. Then as now it took both strong leadership and effective management to make for a successful organization, and
Norbert knew well how fortunate he was to have such a capable
lieutenant in Hugh. They had been virtual partners in inventing
Prémontré, and among other things that meant Norbert had no
qualms whatsoever in leaving, even for months at a time.

One of those journeys came in the spring of 1122. It would
take Norbert back across the Rhine to the Westphalia region of
his home country, to meet with a young prince who would significantly propel the future of the nascent Premonstratensians.
Count Godfrey of Cappenberg was among the highest-ranking
nobles in Germany; just in his early twenties, he had already
inherited great estates and a mantle of political influence.
Though related to Henry V, Godfrey had crossed the emperor
in the Investiture Controversy. The year before, the count had
even taken up arms with other lords in the region against imperial forces in Muenster, thereby putting himself and his family

in grave danger. But his pro-reform position was consistent for Godfrey, a highly sensitive and charitable young man.

Godfrey seems to have been in contact with Norbert at least once before, most likely when the older man was in Cologne acquiring relics and preaching. In any case, sobered by war and imperial politics, trying to make sense of his own purpose in the world, and burdened by guilt over the fiery destruction of the Muenster cathedral during the earlier battle, Godfrey entered a period of deep reflection, and in time he devised a remarkable proposal that he now laid out for Norbert. The count's home was the imposing Cappenberg castle, a hilltop fortress with commanding views in all directions. Godfrey proposed to give Norbert the castle, and a variety of other estates, if he would convert this strategic military redoubt into a Premonstratensian foundation. In this way the gesture called to mind the gift that resulted in the second Norbertine abbey at Floreffe. But here's what made this situation even more dramatic: the powerful count of Cappenberg not only wished to divest of all his worldly holdings; he wanted to join Norbert's community himself.

This was a complicated proposition. As Godfrey had been working out his plan, his young wife, Judith—herself a highborn noble—was not particularly enamored of it. Nor was Godfrey's brother and fellow count, Otto. The region's other lords were up in arms when they learned of it, and the local bishop was opposed too, since the castle was essential to his own security. Finally, Judith's father, Count Frederick of Arnsberg, was violently opposed. A legendary warrior, he swore to take the castle back, by force if necessary. It seems Norbert—by now Godfrey's spiritual adviser as well as prospective beneficiary—was Godfrey's only real encourager. Even so, as Norbert fully grasped the fraught politics of the situation, it's unlikely he would have offered his support if he hadn't been sure of Godfrey's conviction. And in fact, the young man's perseverance was such that, after much discussion, Judith and Otto not only came around to Godfrey's view but agreed to enter the Norbertine community *with* him. Norbert would grow so enamored of Cappenberg that he made himself its provost, or titular head. But in doing so he was also surely wielding his prestige to help protect his vulnerable new foundation.

Given the extraordinary sensitivities and the very real potential for violence, Norbert felt that Godfrey must reconcile with the emperor and secure his blessing. Fortunately, the fall of 1122 had witnessed the Concordat of Worms, in which Henry and the Church finally hit on a compromise that each could live with and thus, at last, bring to an end the fight over investiture. With Henry again in Rome's good graces, Norbert and Godfrey obtained an audience with the emperor, after which he blessed Godfrey's gift of Cappenberg castle to Norbert and his intention to join the Premonstratensian community. (As the exact timing of this meeting is uncertain, some historians have even posited that Norbert perhaps helped persuade Henry to accept the investiture accord, though there is no definitive evidence of that.) Henry's blessing aside, the irate Frederick of Arnsberg was true to his threat: His men set siege to the Cappenberg castle-turned-abbey. The few clerics Norbert had installed there, terrified and readying themselves as martyrs to their cause, managed to get out a message to their superior. Norbert, in the peacemaking way that had been so effective for him elsewhere, decided he would go to Frederick, alone, and try to turn his heart—this despite Frederick's colorful and widely broadcast boast that if he ever got his hands on Norbert, he would hang both the holy man and his donkey from one of his castle rafters to "to see which was heavier." Norbert was undeterred. Yet even as he was on his way to this unpromising summit there occurred another of those remarkable coincidences that seem to have delineated Norbert's life like mile markers. Frederick, while presiding over a large feast, pitched over at his own dinner table in a violent seizure. He died—and so did the final obstacle to the establishment of the Cappenberg community, the first Norbertine foundation in Germany.

Some time later Godfrey took the Norbertine habit. He established a convent at the foot of the Cappenberg castle where Judith, following through on her own spiritual commitment, presided as abbess. His brother Otto also joined the order and donated what would become two other important Norbertine sites, Ilbenstadt and Varlar. For all he had gone through to realize his aspirations, Godfrey, tragically, would serve only a few years before himself succumbing to illness at the age of thirty. But Judith and Otto were blessed with much longer lives, and both contributed important leadership to the emergent Norbertine order.

Even in an age when many nobles were transfixed by religious renewal, the story of the Cappenbergs was extraordinary—that such high-ranking figures would give over not only everything they owned but also their lives to God. Word raced around Europe, and the reputation of Norbert—by now an already well-known figure—began verging on legend. And this, in turn, helped trigger the almost viral growth of his order. "By the strong-willed pursuit of his ideal… [Godfrey] furthered the plans of Norbert more than anybody else," explains Grauwen. "The foundation of Cappenberg and the other monasteries which were established on the estates of the Cappenbergs… meant for Norbert the definitive breakthrough in the spreading of the way of life he had founded." Other magnificent properties would come to be offered up for other foundations; other high-born and landed individuals would give themselves to Norbert's reform cause. Beyond that, some existing religious communities now petitioned to align themselves with the Premonstratensians.

It was not just growth but explosive, head-spinning growth. Importantly, though, it was not growth at any cost. A telling counterpoint to Norbert's experience with Godfrey was one he had at almost the same time with a powerful French prince, Theobald IV. Scion of some of the most noble lines in Europe, grandson of William the Conqueror, Count Theobald controlled vast swaths of France, including the Chartres and Champagne regions; his political influence was rivaled only by that of the French king himself. Another man in his early twenties, Theobald had heard the tales of Norbert and now, in particular, the selfless gestures of the Cappenberg counts. Theobald came to Prémontré not long after all that to meet with Norbert, and after some intense conversations the Frenchman made, in essence, the same offer.

Norbert was of course intrigued by this stunning generosity, but he asked for a few days to consider the idea—and to do the political calculus. Unlike Godfrey, Theobald's dominion was so vast, and his leadership role so prominent, that a move of such magnitude could destabilize all of France. Norbert was also aware that Theobald was a supporter of Church reform and a notably generous ruler for his people. So when they resumed their discussion, Norbert surprised Theobald by saying that God's plan for him was to stay put and continue to help his people— and that included the taking of a wife (Theobald was at that time unmarried) so as to continue the family line and tradition of service. Disappointed but accepting of this verdict, Theobald then surprised Norbert. Since you require me to marry, he said, *you* must find me an appropriate bride! Having so boldly challenged the prince, Norbert could hardly refuse this return challenge. It appears that through his deep Cologne connections Norbert identified the daughter of a German noble as a suitable prospect. Theobald agreed, and he and his wife, Mathilde, would go on to have ten children. A number of their daughters married into royal families; indeed, one would wed the king of France. Theobald would remain close to Norbert and the Premonstratensians for the rest of his life.

As *Vita B* declares in relating the parallel stories of Godfrey and Theobald, "Let the listener consider, therefore, how great the virtue of discretion was in Norbert who, concerning two princes, caused one to give up everything, but ordered the other to possess everything as though having nothing."

Norbert's garden was now growing so quickly that the time

had come for the Church to formally recognize the reality of the situation: The small, remote, one-off community Norbert had established only a few years earlier at Prémontré had not only beaten the odds to survive, but it had spawned a genuine phenomenon. With the loyal confrere Evermode at his side, Norbert took a small delegation to Rome in early 1126. There he received a bull from the pope (now Honorius II) that in essence formally recognized a new Catholic religious order, the Premonstratensians. The papal bull cited eight active foundations—and the Norbertines were just getting started.

CHAPTER 7

THE WONDER WORKER

Encounter by encounter, opportunity by opportunity, foundation by foundation, Norbert was building something robust and special—and new.

In addition to his from-scratch creation at Prémontré, his adaptation of existing churches at Floreffe, his conversion of the onetime Cappenberg fortress (and what would become its brother communities), Norbert, in a creative burst of just a few years, established a number of seminal sites that would anchor the Premonstratensian order for many centuries. Not only did this expedited acquisition and development represent growth that any modern CEO would envy, it also revealed Norbert's talent—genius, really—for adapting. He took on each foundation as the individual entity it was, with its peculiar history and the unique expectations of its patron, and made it work.

Put another way, the growing Premonstratensian order was anything but cookie-cutter. Perhaps this was to be expected from a leader who considered his order more an organic movement than a planned, clearly thought-out organization. For instance, just a short time before Norbert had stumbled onto his opportunity at Prémontré, a small group of clerics had banded together around a beloved priest in another village in the Laon region. Then in 1122, at Bishop Bartholomew's urging, the group threw in with Norbert and became the double monastery of Cuissy, a foundation that would thrive for nearly seven centuries (eventually being extinguished during the French Revolution) and which was famed for the superior quality of its illuminated manuscripts. A few years after using his influence at Cuissy, Bartholomew turned again to Norbert to help with the continuing vexation in his own backyard: St. Martin's collegiate church. Together they converted the Laon church to a Norbertine institution in 1124, with Norbert sending a dozen confreres and installing as the first superior there Walter of Saint-Maurice—one of the seven young men he had recruited for Prémontré from the Laon academy just a few years before. St. Martin's in just over a decade would count more than five hundred religious, men and women. Similarly, Norbert would soon be prevailed upon to take control of a failed canonry in Antwerp, in Belgium, which would go on to become the mighty St. Michael's Abbey.

It was largely through this rapid expansion that Norbert's ostensibly canonical order with the decidedly monastic bent at last began working more seriously with parishes. As indicated previously, Floreffe came with the auxiliary gift of several small churches and thus was established with parish responsibilities from the outset. At remote Prémontré, on the other hand, things had developed more slowly. As the institution established farms farther and farther from the abbey proper and as workers went out to stay permanently, Norbertines soon followed to live and work amongst them—settlements that eventually became parishes. Cuissy's very origins were in serving the people. As St. Martin's and St. Michael's grew within their respective cities, so did the ministry obligations of their canons. And when eventually Norbert would be dispatched to Magdeburg, in far-off eastern Germany, he would adapt again and put parish work at the forefront of this new Premonstratensian frontier.

Another of Norbert's core characteristics revealed by the early growth of his order was his savvy entrepreneurialism. As more and more gifts of major property came to him to establish foundations, Norbert whenever possible got the properties signed over to him *personally*. That wasn't to enrich himself, of course; it was all about control. Primarily he wanted to protect the new foundations from the clutches of local bishops, who in the past tended to wield authority over the religious orders in their dioceses. This was not only politically shrewd on Norbert's part but it represented a radically new concept in the canonical world. No doubt the impulse owed both to Norbert's sophisticated upbringing in imperial courts and to the rough-and-tumble clerical politics he had observed, and endured.

While Norbert's flexibility made pragmatic sense, it also meant his early order was developing an offbeat look and feel. And like anything new, that uniqueness only quickened the drumbeat of criticism from Norbert's naysayers, who watched his mission unfold with growing distaste—and maybe a little envy. Many in the Benedictine and Cistercian world, for instance, scolded him for in essence adulterating the contemplative model—looking and acting a lot like a monastery, but adopting practices (intensive study, parish ministries, preaching) that were anathema to the cloister. On the other hand, fellow canons looked at the Premonstratensians and were irritated by their acceptance of lay participants, as well as what they considered unsanctioned deviations from liturgical and prayer practices. "The canons insisted Norbertines were not canons; the monks were equally certain that they were not monks," sums up an American Norbertine commentary on the early days of the order. "Perhaps nothing could better illustrate the originality and exact nature of the foundation so well as these criticisms."

Contemplating what Norbert accomplished from our twenty-first century vantage point and a world that has made heroes of business visionaries, we come away with a strong appreciation for his many extraordinary leadership qualities— his fearlessness, his opportunism, his ambition, his communication skills. But in Norbert's own time these were not the kinds of qualities that caused "real people" to chatter. The common folk knew about Norbert too—but in their case it was mostly Norbert the healer, the dispatcher of Satan, the anti-heretic, the latter-day apostle. It was this period when Norbert was building his legend, getting as close as an early twelfth-century ascetic could to fame.

IN THE MEDIEVAL CONTEXT of Norbert's life, faith and medicine (such as it was) were close points on the same spectrum. Faith was as essential to good health as it was to eternal salvation; illnesses were often attributed to failures of character or, in the worst cases, demonic possession. As Norbert made his way around villages and towns to preach, he, like virtually all *wanderpredigers*, did much "healing" of supplicants who came to him with their ailments, whether major or mundane. These transactions would have been so commonplace that, for the most part, they happened off the page, as it were—although, as we will see, the *Vitae* do report on at least one occasion when Norbert apparently performed something like a medical miracle, before hundreds of witnesses.

The gift of prophecy also was ascribed to Norbert. An anecdote in *Vita A* describes a pious woman who visited him while he was seeing family in Laon. She is distraught because she and her husband cannot conceive children and she doesn't know what to do about it. Norbert encourages her to hold to her faith and promises that she will soon bear a son—he would be destined for the clergy, Norbert said—followed by additional children. And so it all came to pass.

The larger point is, for Norbert's followers, including his Premonstratensians, there was absolutely no question about their master's power to channel God, to heal in his name, to vanquish the devil. Here was a man, they knew, who spent an extraordinary amount of time in communion with God, the likes of which normal people did not. And there was no reason to think that relationship was a one-way street: people believed that God used Norbert as his instrument.

One of the most striking things about reading *Vita A* and *Vita B* is the amount of time these quite short biographies devote to what are called the "devil stories." The *Vitae* carry the worshipful tone one would expect of accounts from devoted followers, but in most other regards they are straightforward and fairly factual takes on a life—a rather remarkable life, granted, but a mortal one nevertheless. In general there is a staid, unhysterical quality to the narratives. But then every few chapters the authors step back and provide sometimes harrowing anecdotes about Norbert and/or his associates doing battle with Satan. In fact this happens a dozen times or more—enough for the devil to effectively play a supporting character. Meantime, Norbert's fearsome devil-fighting prowess became a major contributor to his popular reputation. Word got around.

The devil stories fall into several categories. There are Norbert's head-to-head confrontations. There are various exorcisms Norbert performs. And finally, there are many accounts of how the devil chronically torments the Prémontré community, almost like a juvenile prankster run amok.

Tellingly, many of these last visitations occur when Norbert is away from Prémontré on his preaching-recruiting missions. It seems no sooner is "Father Norbert" (as he is often called) out the door when the devil invariably turns up, and he does so in many guises. In one instance he appears with three heads, to mock the notion of the Holy Trinity. At other times he turns up as a wolf threatening the flock or masquerades as an angel. He putrefies the community's water supply with a dead toad. He tempts the confreres, he provokes them—sometimes even physically attacks them. The *Vitae* include these stories for a variety of purposes. First, since the *Vitae* were written relatively soon after Norbert's death, the authors almost certainly believed that the devil stories literally happened; they were regarded as an important part of the Norbertine history. But on a more subtle level, they are so heavily reiterated as to leave no doubt about the power of Norbert: that the founder was also the order's great protector, and that he had special, divinely conferred power over evil.

Modern readers, however, take away another, more poignant, meaning from the stories. They help us appreciate what extraordinary hardships the Prémontré community must have faced in those first harsh days. All those strangers huddling there in the spooky woods, in the dark and cold, with danger always lurking nearby and drudgery the order of their day: It's easy to see how a collective psychosis could take hold among them, especially when their leader was gone, and give rise to demon reveries. It seemed everything was conspiring to thwart them—even the Prince of Darkness personally. One reads the stories and feels more than anything a tremendous sympathy for these pioneers and the many obstacles they faced simply to survive. Little wonder they often felt hexed!

These stories also reflect medieval society's utter obsession with demons. "From this series of devil stories...one can draw up a complete demonology for the twelfth century," writes Grauwen in his analysis of these phenomena.

One of the more dramatic of the head-on encounters between Norbert and the devil occurs in what the Premonstratensians call "The Bear Story." In it, Norbert has shuttered himself inside the tiny St. John the Baptist chapel for a night of solitary reflection. Suddenly he senses he is no longer alone. Turning, he is confronted by what, in the faint light, he makes out to be a bear, ominously flashing its teeth and claws. The beast initially terrifies Norbert. Then, as he realizes that he had heard no sound of entry, Norbert understands that he is in the presence of his relentless nemesis. According to the *Vitae* he summons his courage, declaring: "What do you want, you bloody beast? Your claws are without substance, your frightful teeth are air, and your hairy pelt empty smoke and vapor.... . Depart now, I command you, because there is nothing in common between Christ and Belial [the devil], between light and darkness, between the faithful and the unfaithful. Depart quickly! You know you can harm no one without permission...."

Thus chastened, "The liar disappeared," the *Vitae* say, "unable to endure the truth."

The *Vitae* recount three or four of these Norbert-devil confrontations, starkly etched battles between good and evil. We get a similar number of examples of Norbert conducting exorcisms in his travels, and these are related in often harrowing detail. One of the most vivid describes Norbert's exorcism of the devil from a twelve-year-old girl who had been possessed for a year. The preacher had come to the Belgian town of Nivelles, when in desperation the girl's father brings her to the holy man. After Norbert begins reading prayers over her, the devil mocks him by having the child—as innocent as she was illiterate—recite in Latin Solomon's erotically tinged Song of Songs from beginning to end. Then she did so, word for word, in French; and then again in German. Their battle goes back and forth, with the girl at one point seizing Norbert's stole in an effort to strangle him. Those witnessing the exorcism move to retrieve the garment from her, but Norbert halts them. "Don't!" he shouts. "If she has received the power from God, let her do what she can!" With that, she releases her grip.

Things continue in this vein the rest of the day, as the long story takes on the tenor of an evenly matched heavyweight fight. Evening falls with Norbert making no apparent headway, and he returns to his room, discouraged. But after praying for inspiration, he decides that he will not eat until she is cured. At dawn the next day, a great crowd gathers at the church for Norbert's daily Mass. The possessed girl is brought back and placed near the altar, held there firmly by two of Norbert's confreres. The devil continues to mock Norbert through the liturgy's prayers, but at the consecration, when the priest holds aloft the host, the demon begins to relent, thrashing in agony. "Behold, I'm burning! I'm burning!" he cries out through the girl. "Behold, I'm dying! I want to leave!" And with that he is gone at last, leaving only a foul smell in his wake. The exhausted child is healed.

Norbert as protector, Norbert as father, Norbert as healer, Norbert as worker of miracles, Norbert as the devil's worst nightmare. The legend grew.

BUT FOR NORBERT'S critics, that legend only meant more ammunition. It wasn't just other religious orders that had Norbert in their crosshairs. For instance, he somehow managed to find himself the target of a long-running dispute with the French theologian and rationalist Peter Abelard. Philosophy and theology students will recognize Abelard as the brilliant but proud Catholic thinker whose theories, especially as to the nature of the Trinity, increasingly put him at odds with Rome. (Literature students are more likely to recognize him from the celebrated Heloise and Abelard medieval love story, but that is a tale for another book.) The clash may date to 1121 and a synod in Soissons, France, whose purpose was to scrutinize Abelard's views. Soissons is just a little south of Prémontré, and a friend of Norbert's was a bishop there. Some biographers maintain that Norbert was summoned there to refute Abelard's teachings—which would be an ironic turnabout from Norbert's own experience at Fritzlar, if he actually did speak against Abelard at Soissons. (There seems to be no concrete proof that he did.) Nevertheless, Abelard, a committed monastic, would remain a persistent critic of the canon Norbert, whom he considered not only wrongheaded but sanctimonious. He sarcastically labeled Norbert one of the "new apostles" of the age, the rationalist ridiculing the *wanderprediger* as a self-proclaimed miracle worker and con artist.

Norbert's contemporary and great friend Bernard of Clairvaux was much more associated with opposition to Abelard than Norbert ever was, and one wonders if to some extent Norbert didn't suffer at Abelard's hands from that connection. Certainly Norbert didn't overtly set himself against Abelard, and in truth both men were driven by similar convictions, such as their demand for clerical reform. But Abelard simply didn't appreciate how Norbert was going about it—or maybe the acclaim he was receiving in the process. Grauwen nicely encapsulates part of this paradox. "It is clear…that Norbert was generally known as a wonder worker," he writes. "According to Abelard, however, this reputation was not obtained accidentally, but consciously pursued from ambition. Hence his mordant sarcasm. Here two worlds face each other. On the one side you have almost the entire twelfth century society, which demanded miracles, and Norbert, who was probably convinced of his power to work miracles. And on the other side is the critical Abelard, in this respect an exception to his time, who denounced everything as intended deceit and ambition."

What we do know is that this age provoked a great mixing of ideas, and great passions that attended them. The same issues that had catalyzed the Gregorian reform movement throughout Norbert's life (e.g., the investiture crisis, corrupt practices, clergy who were more selfish than selfless) also gave rise to many fierce opponents of the Church, whose teachings it deemed heretical. One of the most successful—and most notorious, at least at the time—of these was a charismatic preacher named Tanchelm (also known as Tanchelin). Around 1100 Tanchelm, a putative monk of shadowy background, began working in areas of present-day Holland and the Low Countries. As his teachings and personal behavior grew more hostile to the Church, both religious and secular authorities began to hound him and sent him on the run. In 1115—the same year as Norbert's conversion, interestingly—Tanchelm was assaulted and killed by an enraged Catholic priest, but not before he had turned many thousands of believers to his cause. Among other things, Tanchelm denied the authority of the pope and the clergy—and because the latter were thought to be unworthy conduits, he maligned the sacraments as well. In particular he discounted the Eucharist, rejecting the Church's teaching that the Communion host is transubstantiated into the real presence of Christ.

As it happened, Tanchelm had found a singularly receptive audience in the Belgian port city of Antwerp. Driven by trade, Antwerp was growing fast, but at this time it was still just one parish served by a lone church, St. Michael's, which had the additional disadvantage of being some distance from the city center. Compounding things, the canons of St. Michael's concerned themselves only with their liturgical functions and not at all with pastoral care or outreach. Conditions were ripe for a disrupter like Tanchelm to make a mark, and nearly a decade after his death Tanchelm's cult remained firmly entrenched in Antwerp. This was especially problematic to the Church, given that Antwerp was not only a prosperous city but an influential one, since so many things—including ideas—came and went through it.

At this time Antwerp belonged to the huge diocese of Cambrai, whose bishop was Norbert's associate Burchard. Frustrated by his related problems there—the inert canonry at St. Michael's and the strong grip that Tanchelm still had—Burchard had a brainstorm. He made the pilgrimage to Prémontré, where he asked his old friend for help. Come to Antwerp and eradicate the memory of Tanchelm, Burchard said—and while you're at it, please take over St. Michael's as your next Premonstratensian foundation. At this point and under normal circumstances, Norbert might well have been disinclined to begin another monastery so far from home and in a large city. Yet he could scarcely turn down the man who, only a few years earlier, literally saved his life.

So it was that in 1123 Norbert took a small party of his most trusted confreres and set out for Antwerp. Once there, he actually found a ready audience, people who wanted to listen out of a mixture of curiosity (his fame having by then reached the North Sea) and perhaps guilt for having so readily embraced a theology they suspected was counterfeit. In any case, when Norbert took the pulpit, he quickly sized up his audience and neither chastised nor rebuked. Instead, he put across a message of sympathy and understanding. "Brothers, do not be surprised and do not be afraid," Norbert said, according to an account in *Vita B*. "Unwittingly, you have pursued falsehood thinking it to be the truth. If you had been taught the truth first, you would have been found effortlessly tending toward salvation, just as you now effortlessly lean toward perdition."

From the start it was clear the people of Antwerp had been starving for such priestly understanding and consideration. In the next weeks and months Norbert continued his ministrations in this vein, as did his Premonstratensian companions, and their charitable approach resonated with the believers of Antwerp. "Many of them, when they came to confession, brought consecrated hosts that they had been keeping hidden in boxes and odd corners of their houses for years," writes Campbell.

Per their arrangement, Burchard would turn over St. Michael's to Norbert, and within a few short decades it would have more than five hundred confreres and be one of the most influential abbeys in the order. Norbert himself, meanwhile, would come to be hailed as the Apostle of Antwerp.

IT WILL BE RECALLED that almost from the beginning at Prémontré, Norbert had made a priority of erecting a new church for his first community. And he did so out of his usual combination of divine inspiration—according to the order's tradition, the building site was picked based on a vision that one of the Norbertine brothers had conveyed to Norbert—and native ingenuity. As to that latter point: Because speed was of the essence, Norbert arranged for both local French and imported German stonemasons to work on the primary construction, appreciating that the natural and longstanding rivalry between the two groups would spur them to try to outdo one another. In fact, he assigned the French workers one side of the church and the Germans the other, setting up a virtual race.

The only problem was that as soon as the builders set to their work they realized that Norbert's divinely inspired site was one no engineer would have selected. It was too marshy for heavy construction and required load after load of rock fill to make for an adequate foundation. Nevertheless, by all accounts the erection of the church seems to have come along fairly quickly—if not finished, at least to the point where it could be consecrated by the fall of 1122. But at the dedication Mass, when it came time for the offertory, hundreds from the large audience apparently crowded around the altar, as was a customary practice at the time. Their focused load must have caused some kind of shift in the suspect foundation beneath their feet, for the altar also slipped somewhat and was said to have "cracked."

From a canonical standpoint, the damage to the altar meant the dedication ceremony had to stop; the consecration was deemed invalid. Before long the foundation would be shored up and a new altar placed, and a second consecration was quietly carried out. The more important implication, however, was metaphysical. In the medieval age it was a given that such signs came from God and had a reason, which was for the mortals to interpret. In the immediate aftermath, Norbert fretted about what we might call the public relations aspect, the fear of "the scandal that might be caused among the weaker and more superstitious spirits," writes Campbell. But Norbert, experiencing the rare moment of discouragement, wondered more privately about what the omen of a broken altar meant.

He determined, ultimately, that it was an indication that "in the future this should be performed anew," writes Grauwen. He shared this interpretation with his Norbertine confidantes. The *Vitae* are opaque on whether Norbert meant by this the new altar consecration, which did happen soon after, or the replacement of the entire church—which also would come to pass, not terribly long after his death, in yet another effort to try to stay abreast of the tremendous growth of the Prémontré community.

However, given Norbert's mystical belief in premonition and God's plan for him, one can also reasonably wonder if he didn't read it as a sign that what might be "performed anew" was his own life. If so, the premonition would soon prove correct.

CHAPTER 8

THE ARCHBISHOP

Pope Gregory VII, catalyst of the great Church reform movement that would span Norbert's entire life, had died in 1085. His papacy lasted twelve years, and Norbert was still a boy when it ended. As it happened, a number of Gregory's immediate successors to the throne of St. Peter would occupy it for short durations. Five different popes would rule between Norbert's conversion experience in 1115 and the end of his own life, and four of these faced antipopes—competitors set up by opposing factions—who tried to undermine their legitimacy. Antipopes were common in the early Church, in particular through the medieval period.

Such a fraught state of Church leadership affected all faithful Catholics, of course, but for someone like Norbert, whose life's work depended almost entirely on papal approvals, the situation must have been especially vexing.

When in early 1126 Norbert ventured again to Rome, this time to secure the first charters of the Premonstratensian order, the pope was Honorius II. A humble-born but brilliant executive in the Gregorian mold, Honorius had only recently succeeded Norbert's patron Callixtus. Honorius was a supporter

of the newer clerical orders in the Church, and as such he welcomed Norbert warmly and gave his fulsome approval to the
Premonstratensians. Even before Norbert's visit, the pope would
have known about him due to the rapid rise and spread (not
to mention the uniqueness) of his new order, but like so many
other Catholics he probably also had heard the tales of Norbert
the preacher, healer and devil's adversary. All indications are the
two men got on very well. In addition to making his case with
Honorius for the Premonstratensian foundations, Norbert
also spent time with him discussing the need for ongoing
clerical reform, notably in the company of another distinguished
German, the theologian Gerhoh of Reichersberg. Though
Norbert's stay in Rome was relatively brief—four to six weeks at
most—it was time enough for Honorius to form a substantial,
and positive, impression of one of his more iconoclastic servants,
this man who seemed to be equal parts wandering preacher and
empire-builder.

While in Rome Norbert also played the tourist, visiting various martyr sites and saintly tombs. But as soon as he was able
he headed back for Prémontré. He took a more easterly route, by
way of Germany, to tend to some obligations and to follow up on
some opportunities; it was on this leg, for instance, that he would
strike agreements for several more German additions to the
order. Even so, Norbert, per his custom, preached everywhere
he went. Just in time for Holy Week he arrived in Wuerzburg, an
important city about fifty miles southeast of Frankfurt that was
then mourning the recent death of its bishop. In the prelate's
absence the community invited their esteemed visitor to preside

over the Easter High Mass at the cathedral. According to the *Vitae*, it was during this Mass, after Communion, that the packed assembly watched as a blind woman was led to the altar and cried out for Norbert to heal her. Norbert, moved by her plight as well as her faith, approached the woman and gently breathed across her closed eyes; when she opened them, the legend tells us, she could see.

It was an electric moment that made Wuerzburg's embrace of Norbert all the more feverish—so much so that sentiment quickly arose to keep him there as the next bishop. This talk so disconcerted Norbert that he slipped away while he still could. Besides, after so long an absence from Prémontré, he longed to be back at the place that, by now, he considered home. He finally reached his charter community in late May of 1126.

But it seems Wuerzburg was not the only diocese in Germany then in need of new leadership. During his journey to Rome, Norbert learned that the archbishopric of Magdeburg, in far-off eastern Germany, had recently opened too, and some months had already passed with no clear favorite emerging from several candidates being considered. And whoever did get the posting would face a unique challenge. Strictly from an ecclesiastical standpoint Magdeburg was not especially important, given its location on what might be called the Christian frontier. Just to the east of Magdeburg, across the Elbe River, were the Wends, a Slavic people who stubbornly maintained their pagan beliefs and practices. Their prospective conversion was a primary reason for Magdeburg's establishment in the first place—though little actual missionary activity had occurred.

Yet for all its remoteness, Magdeburg could claim a rich political and economic heritage. "For centuries Magdeburg had played an important role in the German empire," writes A.W. van den Hurk, "as it was for the east what Aachen was in the west"—which is to say its history was intertwined with that of the empire. In the tenth century, Otto the Great had made Magdeburg the imperial capital, building a cathedral there and establishing the archbishopric. He also invested the holder of that see with considerable secular power; the archbishop was expected to be a trusted personal adviser. Magdeburg was a gateway for trade, as well. Still, by this point in the early twelfth century, the city's sunnier days were considered to be behind it. Magdeburg's pedigree notwithstanding, a future archbishop might have had to look hard to ascertain its appeal.

No sooner had Norbert returned to his routine at Prémontré when circumstances tugged at him to leave again. Count Theobald had come personally to ask Norbert to accompany him back to Germany to finalize the arrangements for his marriage to Mathilde. On the face of it, that was the last thing Norbert wished to do. He and Hugh were still catching up on developments at Prémontré during his absence, and, more important, they were now deep into discussions of how best to manage a Norbertine organization that was exploding in size and geographic reach. It had become obvious that it was physically impossible, and perhaps philosophically unwise, for one person—even one as inventive and energetic as Norbert—to try to direct day-to-day operations across such a far-flung enterprise. Thus the idea of leaving Prémontré again so quickly was unappealing. But Norbert had little choice. After all, he was the one who had insisted Theobald marry in the first place and then found him a suitable bride; he could now scarcely decline the count's invitation to secure the sacrament.

According to Norbertine tradition, however, there was another good reason for Norbert's reticence to leave, and especially for Germany. The *Vitae* tell us that shortly before Norbert was set to depart Rome, he was meditating with his confreres before dawn one day. Suddenly they heard a disembodied voice, and it proclaimed that Norbert would, that same year, become the bishop of "Parthenopolis"—Greek for what the group took to be Magdeburg. All clearly heard the voice and the prediction, and they were all said to be so shaken by it that they didn't speak of it again. Norbert himself would confide the encounter to only a handful of intimates. Yet he carried the premonition back to Prémontré, where it weighed on him relentlessly. And now, he feared, a return to Germany might tempt fate too well.

Nonetheless, Norbert, while uncertain where this trip would actually take him, made ready to journey with Theobald. As he did so, he tried to quell the sensation that he might never be back. Still, he called together his charter community and, in what they must have assumed would be just another bit of fatherly instruction, instead gave them a broader exhortation—remarks that many would later interpret as a kind of valedictory address. They didn't realize it at the time, of course, as Norbert didn't let on that anything about this moment was different. Indeed, we don't even know with certainty that the address even happened. Yet it came to be a signal event in Norbertine tradition, and it is well described by Norbertine author Cornelius Kirkfleet. In his account, Norbert tells his followers to be "most diligent in the service of God" and reminds them that they are "obliged daily to carry the cross of Christ." He continued:

> This, indeed, is the narrow road to heaven, our true country. This is the road which Jesus Christ has pointed out to us by his life and his death, his words and his deeds, and which infallibly leads to their heavenly country all who persevere to the end in that path. You cannot go to Christ unless you enter upon this narrow road with courage and confidence, and do your best to follow it. An apostle has said, "For he also that striveth for the mastery, is not crowned except he strive lawfully." And another: "He that saith he abideth in him ought himself also to walk, even as [Christ] walked."

Norbert encouraged his people to only leave the monastery when they absolutely must, lest they miss out on the gratification of communal life or be tempted by the wickedness awaiting outside the walls. "Love the cloister," he said, "which protects you and keeps the mind pure." Likewise did he admonish them to "watch over your tongue" so as not to upset the "sweet peace" of the community, and to accept the inevitable aches and pains visited on them as transitory obstacles on their journey to Christ.

He closed his admonition with the ideas of selflessness and sacrifice and the example of Christ's original disciples—which, considering these were the main reasons they had followed

Norbert to Prémontré in the first place, surely resonated with everyone who heard the address:

> Endeavor, therefore, to avoid the terrible judgments of God by constantly doing his will in fear and righteousness, in order that God may keep you in holy religion, and that in his mercies he may preserve you from everlasting punishment in hell. God will abundantly reward those who are faithful in his service, for God gives a great reward for a small service, as he himself promised his disciples, who having abandoned all they had, asked what should be their reward: "You shall receive a hundredfold and possess life everlasting."

Norbert took in this assemblage he had labored so hard to build and had instructed countless times. "May Jesus Christ lead you there," he said to them. "Amen."

SO IT WAS THAT in June 1126 Norbert took leave of his beloved Prémontré. Theobald's entourage was to rendezvous with Mathilde's bridal party at a prearranged location near the French and German border. When Theobald and Norbert arrived, however, they were met with sober news: Mathilde was said to be seriously ill. In fact, she was still back in Regensburg, an influential Bavarian outpost about fifty miles north of Munich. Theobald was distraught at this turn of events—and his concern was no doubt exacerbated by the suspicions of some in his traveling party that what Mathilde really had was cold feet. Understandably, Theobald needed to ascertain the truth of the matter, and he trusted only one person for the job.

Norbert again acceded to his protégé's request, this time heading off for Regensburg. His route eastward would take him through the city of Speyer, where he would cross the Rhine. But once he arrived there, Norbert's journey was interrupted—in every conceivable sense.

At that very moment, the new head of the Holy Roman Empire, Lothair III, was in Speyer too, leading a convocation of German princes and bishops. Several cardinals attended as legates of Honorius, as well as a delegation of officials from Magdeburg, who were hoping to settle the still-open question of the city's next archbishop. Lothair, who had assumed the imperial throne a year earlier upon the death of Henry V, was considered more faithful to the Church, and his elevation had the pope's blessing. The Easter before—at the same time Norbert was healing the blind woman in Wuerzburg—Lothair had been in Magdeburg, trying to resolve the open episcopate. Several prominent candidates were debated, but when no one of them rose clearly to the top the emperor deferred the matter until the upcoming Diet of Speyer.

Once the celebrated Norbert arrived in Speyer—the recent miracle at Wuerzburg was only the latest exploit of his now in wide circulation—word raced around the city. According to the standard account, the authorities took advantage of his "surprise" presence to invite Norbert to give the diet's opening sermon. Norbert made it a pointed one. With his usual eloquence and passion he spoke "on the duties of Christian rulers and their subjects, on the government of the Church and the election of bishops," writes Campbell. Afterward Norbert was anxious to continue on to Regensburg, but Lothair himself is said to have asked the holy man to stay in Speyer a while longer.

A few days later, then, the diet reopened the Magdeburg discussion. Two candidates were carryovers from the Eastertide debate. But a murmur rippled through the assembly when a surprise third name, a new one, was now put into nomination—that of Norbert. According to the legend, no one was more surprised than the nominee himself. Indeed, Norbert was reportedly horrified to be watching his premonition unfold precisely as he'd feared. Nonetheless, deliberations continued until at last one of the other candidates stood and proclaimed to the assembly that the man they should elect was right there—pointing at Norbert. The rest of the assembly then rose as well and offered a general acclamation. Stunned, Norbert protested to Lothair and the papal legates that he wasn't worthy, didn't wish it, couldn't possibly be the one. No matter. The emperor endorsed the call, as did the papal legates, one of whom then made it official. "We, in the name of the Father and of the Son and of the Holy Spirit, elect and name as your bishop the Lord Norbert, a man of proved virtue," he declared. "We are convinced that it was for this very purpose that God brought him here."

Lothair installed Norbert on the spot, the papal legates pressing into the *wanderprediger*'s leathery hands the shepherd's crozier. He was then instructed to travel to Magdeburg without delay to take up his new duties. Norbert protested that at the very least he must first go to Regensburg to sort out matters with Mathilde, but he was dissuaded even of that; Theobald's envoy, it seems, would have to send an envoy of his own. (Mathilde, it turns out, had recovered and, as we have seen, wed the count after all.)

WHAT LITTLE WE ACTUALLY know about the "drafting" of Norbert to the See of Magdeburg comes mostly from his *Vitae*—and frankly, those lightly sketched accounts raise far more questions than they answer. The abrupt departure of Norbert from Prémontré to become an archbishop is one of the most enigmatic developments in a life full of them. Was this truly another example of providence, a divinely inspired foregone conclusion, something essentially beyond Norbert's control? Or might it have been an outcome Norbert secretly wanted?

The answer to the first question is unknowable, of course, but as to the second, it's fair to wonder. Consider the man and consider his circumstances. Norbert had always been ambitious, always antsy, always anxious to embrace the "next big thing," whatever that might prove to be. One of Norbert's few constants, A.W. van den Hurk reminds us, was contradiction. "There is no one straight line or direction in Norbert's life," he writes. "His conceptions adapted and changed with the changing circumstances in his life." Indeed, by this point Norbert was already making plans with Hugh of Fosse to reorder and distribute management authority over the Premonstratensian abbeys, a situation that would leave the founder with far fewer direct responsibilities—and thus, perhaps, open to new pursuits. And Norbert's core interests would have been markedly different from those of the more traditional candidates for the archbishopric; for instance, despite Magdeburg's less appealing aspects, Norbert might well have seen it as a promising opportunity to advance his reform agenda and, frankly, continue to grow the Premonstratensian reach across Germany and beyond. At the same time, the onetime courtier would have appreciated the political clout that could come from the See of Magdeburg, especially if—as the confident Norbert would expect—he was able to gain the trust of his new patron, Lothair. And that connection, in turn, would have gone a long way to help protect Norbert's order, which in its adolescence remained vulnerable—and would be even more so with the founder out of the picture. This paternal instinct surely was one of Norbert's key motivations.

So one can envision a number of reasons Norbert might have been tempted by this prospect. Then you have to look at the highly curious way events unfolded. The series of "coincidences" that landed Norbert in Speyer just as Lothair's episcopal deliberations were getting under way strain credulity. Beyond that, if Norbert dreaded the prospect of the bishop's miter so much, why didn't he find a way to duck the spotlight rather than seize it and speak so pointedly on the "duties of Christian rulers" and "the government of the Church"—in effect, audition for the job? No, the far more likely scenario is that this was all an elaborately choreographed opportunity to get Norbert into the right position before the right people at the right time. Pope Honorius had probably already decided he wanted Norbert in Magdeburg, and yet Norbert would still have to demonstrate his worthiness to Lothair, as they were virtual strangers. That is the view of Grauwen, who has researched his order's founder more deeply than anyone else—and who, throughout his work, respectfully but unflinchingly strips away the centuries of hagiography that cloud our view of the flesh-and-blood Norbert. Having scoured the available documentary evidence of the Speyer conference and sifted the Norbert legend through the historical facts and context, Grauwen concludes that "all this seems to strengthen the hypothesis that there was no coincidence at play, but rather the normal finish of a preconceived plan that had probably been made in February 1126 at Rome"—that is, when Norbert was meeting with Honorius and other top Church officials. Indeed, having been so impressed with Norbert, Honorius might well have judged the German-born ascetic an apt and trustworthy (especially where Rome was concerned) partner for the new German king. Too, it was still the case that bishops typically came from the aristocracy. And if Norbert a decade earlier had turned his back on his secular life, he was still an aristocrat, albeit one who often went barefoot and wore the penitent's scratchy wool robe.

It's true this all remains a matter for conjecture; there is no black-and-white evidence that Norbert's selection as archbishop of Magdeburg was the culmination of some secret plan or inevitable progression. On the other hand, it is the nature of secret plans that the protagonists don't talk much about them and thus leave a trail for us to follow. Norbert would have divulged the touchy reality of this situation to only a handful of intimates, if even to them.

And what of the fabled "Parthenopolis" episode? Well, whether the "voice" Norbert heard steering him to Magdeburg belonged to God, or the pope, or the pope's advisers, or simply his own conscience, it scarcely matters now. Certainly the anecdote, like that of Norbert's conversion, is of a piece with the kinds of heavenly interventions routinely cited in saintly turning points. And from a political standpoint, Norbert could well have used a handy cover story to explain how a man who had made his reputation espousing poverty was now about to re-enter the highest levels of privilege. Such a dramatic change was as inconvenient as it was inconsistent.

Of one thing we *can* be fairly sure, both from the *Vitae* and from a basic grasp of human nature: Norbert had deep misgivings about breaking from his community, and he likewise must have worried how this turn would be read by his friends, associates and critics. A career that had taken him from riches to rags was about to return him to riches, or at least the trappings of the rich. As he tried to persuade himself that this was something he could do, or would do, this man of profound faith and reflection surely prayed long hours to God as to whether he *should* do it.

In the end, of course, Norbert had no choice but to do what his emperor and his pope were asking of him—just as he acceded to his superiors a few years earlier when they prevailed on him to settle down and establish a new religious order. But as he did at Prémontré, Norbert could at least endeavor to undertake the assignment on his own terms. Making his entrance at Magdeburg, where a jubilant crowd had gathered to welcome him, Norbert conspicuously arrived in bare feet—a powerful and endearing gesture of humility. And later, when the new archbishop was to attend a reception in his honor, the thin and still somewhat ragged Norbert was stopped by a porter at the cathedral gate, who had mistaken him for a beggar. Several of Norbert's companions were aghast at the gaffe and chastised the porter. Norbert, however, offered the man a wry smile and some reassurance. "Don't be afraid," he said. "You know me better and see me with a clearer eye than those who force me to this palace to which I, poor and simple, ought not be raised."

AT FIRST MAGDEBURG SEEMED elated with Norbert's appointment. In modern parlance he was a good "catch" and the people well knew it. Alas, it was to prove a short-lived honeymoon.

Formally installed to his position that July, Norbert in his customary fashion went right to work. The first order of business was to ascertain why an archdiocese that had been so generously endowed by Otto when it was established now found itself in a such a hand-to-mouth situation. Upon investigation Norbert learned that previous prelates had given much of that patrimony to relatives and associates, while other resources were simply squandered or flat-out stolen. Norbert decided to claw back what he could—not for his own sake, but as a responsible steward for his archdiocese. Norbert's representatives immediately notified the holders of any ill-gotten estates that the property was to be returned to the Church. Local vassals were astonished at this temerity, and most simply ignored the decree. But Norbert didn't flinch. Instead, he pulled out the biggest weapon at his disposal: He excommunicated them. While official separation from God was a profound penalty, the action had earthly implications too. "The consequences of excommunication were serious in those days, entailing severe penalties in civil law," explains Campbell. "After a year they would be outlawed and lose the right to be heard in courts of law." Thus sobered, the holders of the disputed properties began returning them—but not without a deep and lingering resentment.

Meanwhile, Norbert was also starting to make enemies among his clergy. Despite the Church's fairly recent reiteration of its celibacy policy, many priests in the archdiocese were married or maintained mistresses and in general led lives guided more by their own interests than the Church's expectations. Previous bishops, more laissez-faire in their outlook and with much less fealty to Rome, had inculcated this attitude. But Norbert, like a by-the-book army sergeant taking charge of a sloppy unit, made it clear that things were about to change. He declared that the rules on celibacy were forthwith to be enforced. Existing marriages would be invalidated, current mistresses were to be alienated, and in all other ways the priests of Magdeburg were to follow the rules. Those who didn't would forfeit their clerical privileges and benefits. Norbert's inherited priests were not pleased. As Campbell puts it, it was "deeply resented by the clergy as an intolerable imposition that a stranger should come among them and interfere with their ancient customs and established way of life."

For many in Magdeburg, then, the new archbishop, in a stunningly short time, had gone from a godsend to an enemy in their midst. But Norbert didn't especially care—and he wasn't finished.

He would hit another nerve when, in the spring of 1129, he effected a plan that he had been considering from his first days at Magdeburg. He was keen to bring a Premonstratensian presence to the archdiocese, to secure a source of clergy whose rigor, spirituality and loyalty he could count on. At the same time he was extremely concerned about the state of a community of secular canons at the Church of St. Mary, which had been established under imperial decree a century earlier but whose buildings now were dilapidated (some had never been finished at all) and whose clergy were dispirited and impoverished. Norbert quietly secured Lothair's approval to remake St. Mary's into a Premonstratensian community and redistribute its existing canons to other locations around the archdiocese, where they could perhaps be of more use to him. Not surprisingly, when Norbert confided his intentions to the St. Mary's chapter, the men loudly objected. So too did the clergy at Norbert's own cathedral. Both groups considered the plan an outrageous presumption on the part of the new archbishop—a naked power play for his order and an attack on St. Mary's royal lineage. When they appealed to Lothair, however, they were rebuffed, as he fully supported what Norbert wished to do. Thus St. Mary's became the first

Norbertine foundation in Saxony, under Norbert's direct super-
vision as superior. While the cathedral naturally remained the
metropolitan's seat, St. Mary's would always be the place to
which Norbert retreated for respite and spiritual peace, his new
home away from home.

For many in the ranks of Norbert's growing opposition,
the arrival of the White Fathers in Magdeburg represented
both an impudent rebuke and a newly disciplined approach to
ministry they had little interest in. For some, in fact, it was the
final straw—and the apparent trigger for at least three earnest
attempts on Norbert's life, as all three transpired around the
time he was putting into place his plan for St. Mary's (the spring
of 1129) and the details of which are recounted in the *Vitae*.

The first attempt, we learn, came one day when Norbert
was hearing confessions. A young cleric suddenly turned up and
insisted on being heard immediately. Norbert's servant repeatedly told the man he must wait his turn, but this only made
him more agitated. When Norbert finally met with his visitor,
he immediately sensed from the man's anxious demeanor that
something was amiss. He instructed his servants to remove the
man's robe—whereby they found the long knife he was conceal-
ing. Under questioning the cleric admitted that he had been
bribed to murder the archbishop. When Norbert pressed him
further, he was told that the conspirators were administrators in
his own diocesan office. According to the *Vitae*, the day of the
foiled assassination attempt was Holy Thursday—in Christian
tradition the night Judas betrayed Jesus to the authorities.

A second similar attempt soon followed. This time

Norbert and his chaplains were entering the dark cathedral for the evening office. As they did, a cleric said to be from the archbishop's household hid behind a door, dagger in hand. When the last figure in the procession passed by—typically the archbishop—the assassin lunged with his weapon, inflicting a serious, but not fatal, wound. But the victim was not Norbert. On this occasion, for whatever reason, the archbishop was elsewhere in the procession and was unharmed.

Then came a third attempt, which was the most alarming of all as it amounted to a general revolt against Norbert's authority. That June, Norbert had been told that some kind of terrible crime (the particulars are lost to history) had occurred in the cathedral, and under canon law the archbishop felt obligated to reconsecrate it. But in a sign of how at odds Norbert was at that moment with the cathedral's chapter, the canons disagreed with him utterly. The matter was debated and debated to no avail, until at last one night Norbert quietly took several of his suffragan bishops and a few loyal canons into the cathedral and performed the reconsecration ceremony. As they were finishing, however, an angry mob arrived, having been tipped off by Norbert's most ardent enemies and inflamed by false rumors that his true intent was to rummage the cathedral. As the crowd grew in size and anger, Norbert's much smaller group fled to a fortified tower adjacent to the cathedral. Then at dawn the mob started to assail the tower, some launching arrows and flinging javelins. Another group used a battering ram to get in and managed to reach the top of the tower. In the ensuing skirmish Norbert was struck and one of his servants was wounded by a sword. But we are told that the archbishop, with his persuasive tongue and his peacemaker's skill, somehow managed to mollify the attack band in the tower, even as the local authorities were finally breaking up the larger group outside. But the siege had lasted a full twelve hours and left Norbert no doubt as to the consequences of his reform agenda.

ANXIOUS AS NORBERT WAS to import Premonstratensians to Saxony, as archbishop he had considerably more pastoral concerns to worry about than he did when he was founding a more monastically focused community in the remote environs of Prémontré. In Magdeburg he was responsible for the souls in six subordinate dioceses; he needed priests who were trained and disposed to work with the parishioners. Hard experience had also shown him that it would go better for the Premonstratensians if he permitted some integration with local customs and liturgical practices. For instance, at the Gottesgnaden abbey, located a little south of Magdeburg and founded in 1131, the so-called White Fathers were authorized to wear the black capes of the region's canons. And the German Norbertines were exempted from some of the more austere practices still common back at Prémontré, such as ritual fasting. (Or maybe Norbert was simply just coming around to the view of the St. Martin canons of Laon who, years before, had revolted at their upstart leader's severe expectations of them. "God wants us to mortify ourselves," they had told Norbert, "not kill ourselves.") The point is, Norbert again demonstrated his willingness to bend to the pragmatic in a greater cause.

Yet in his *own* adaptations, he was once more provoking great criticism. The dramatic changes in the circumstances and lifestyle of the famously penniless *wanderprediger* did not escape attention or comment. As archbishop Norbert did try to live frugally, at least relative to the norms of his position. But the fact was that being named the prelate of Magdeburg was more than a spiritual appointment. The archbishop was an official adviser to the emperor and his title was the equivalent of a count. With that eminence came a mansion for a home, horses instead of donkeys, fine linen in place of undyed wool. It also meant that Norbert was often away from his spiritual duties on state business, and as expected he relatively quickly seems to have gained the confidence of Lothair. Coming to Magdeburg essentially returned Norbert to the life of the nobility, and no amount of economizing on the household budget was going to make it seem otherwise to those who watched this change with perplexity, or worse.

Of course, Norbert knew from the outset that his appointment would exert a cost, and it did. Norbert's *Vitae*—unsurprisingly for documents that portray Norbert's election as the fulfillment of a divine plan—don't really discuss Norbert engaging in any overt self-doubt (not that twelfth-century nobles were much given to self-doubt anyway). Still, we can infer from his reaction to the stings of Fritzlar that Norbert must have been sensitive to, and maybe even felt a little guilty about, these fresh accusations of hypocrisy. Some critics went further and accused Norbert of apostasy (the yielding of one's core religious beliefs). How could the man who had preached so far and wide about renunciating one's worldly goods now seemingly embrace them? Some even said that Norbert's followers no longer wished to be called "Norbertines."

We don't know how widespread this internal criticism was, but there is poignant evidence that it existed. Godfrey of Cappenberg, who had given up so much to devote his life to God and for whom Norbert was a beloved spiritual mentor, was called to Magdeburg in the fall of 1126, not long after Norbert had taken up his new role. But by the end of that year he would leave, disillusioned by the changes he had witnessed in his hero. As Grauwen notes, the disillusionment was not because Norbert had become a lesser man, or even a different man. But in his exalted new circumstances there was scant trace of the impoverished, latter-day apostle Godfrey had sworn to emulate. And for such an emotionally sensitive convert, that was everything. As Grauwen puts it, "For the first time [Godfrey] came to the conclusion that his spiritual father was not perfect."

CHAPTER 9

THE COUNSELOR

One of the rare pleasant diversions Norbert experienced during this otherwise anxious period occurred in the summer of 1128, when he was invited back to his hometown, Xanten. In 1109 the town's church, St. Victor, was destroyed in a fire, and soon after a grander replacement for it was begun. By 1128, the choir of the new collegiate church and a number of altars were ready for dedication. (That church wouldn't actually be finished for another four decades—and the work on the majestic cathedral that stands in the center of Xanten today would not begin until 1263.)

As it happened Norbert's former benefactor, Archbishop Frederick of Cologne, was out of favor with Rome as the dedication loomed. Ever the resourceful politician, Frederick had the shrewd insight to ask that Norbert do it instead. Just a dozen years before, this very spot had seen Norbert's first priestly humiliation, when he was literally spat upon by his fellow canons as they turned him aside. Now Norbert was the returning hero, and all was forgiven. Indeed the Xanten canons welcomed him as one of their own, for while he had left them he had never formally resigned from the chapter. One can only imagine

Norbert's joy that July at this ironic turn of events. As he conse-crated the church altars, the now-famous archbishop slowly and devoutly moving among his proud family and friends, Norbert surely must have taken a moment to tally all that he had accom-plished in the improbable years since being driven from his home in disgrace.

But soon enough it was back to Magdeburg, where, all things considered, maybe Norbert's single biggest accomplish-ment as archbishop was staying alive. The violent opposition Norbert faced in the early years of his archbishopric tended to overshadow the many achievements he had realized in what was, after all, a monumental organizational challenge. That shouldn't be surprising given that Norbert was the kind of per-son who was spurred, not cowed, by adversity. And so he pushed on. His insistence on recovering the archdiocese's pilfered prop-erty and imposing fiscal discipline put Magdeburg on a sound footing for the first time in memory. His clerical reforms, though hard fought and as emotionally exhausting for him as for his adversaries, would reverse a long, destructive malaise and help spark a spiritual renewal among his flock. Then there was his important work in regard to the Slavic tribes to the east. It must be remembered that Norbert really wore three distinct hats while serving in Magdeburg—shepherd of that expansive arch-diocese, of course, but also imperial counselor to Lothair and guiding presence for the Premonstratensians. With so much on his plate, he never really had the time to evangelize personally among the Wends, something the preacher in him keenly wished to do. Administratively, however, Norbert did make some major inroads into this longstanding, if largely ignored, priority. From his first days in Magdeburg he worked to reiterate and expand his see's formal authority over that challenging region—sometimes with diplomacy, sometimes by knocking heads. In the process he prepared the ground for what would be the Wends' eventual conversion a few decades later (work done largely by the White Fathers imported by Norbert).

Indeed, Norbert's anticipation of that difficult missionary work across the Elbe was one of the reasons he was so determined to grow the presence of his order in the east. During his tenure in Magdeburg he would establish several nearby Norbertine abbeys, including Gottesgnaden (the gift of a wealthy count who had no heirs) and a former Benedictine monastery called Poehlde that in recent decades had lost its way. As archbishop, however, Norbert's overriding interest was in creating a healthy environment for religious communities generally, not just an opportune one for his own Premonstratensians. As evidence of this, Norbert also authorized two Benedictine monasteries during this same time and grew close to their superiors. Still, the Norbertines' expansion in Saxony only reinforced why a new "global" leadership arrangement for the order was becoming necessary. The Premonstratensians had long since passed the point where they could hang together by the sheer force of Norbert's personal example and charisma. There were too many Norbertines now, geographically too far apart, and there was only one Norbert.

So Norbert and Hugh, after much private discussion and after inviting the input of their institutions' superiors, now made several crucial decisions. The first was to install abbots to run the most significant foundations, such as Floreffe, St. Martin's in Laon, St. Michael's in Antwerp and Viviers in southern France. Once this precedent was established, it would quickly become the order's leadership model. Second, Hugh, who not only continued to personally oversee the Prémontré community, had been elected the first Premonstratensian abbot general, with administrative responsibility over the entire order. (Technically speaking, Hugh was elected by all the order's superiors, but Norbert's desire for this outcome was clear—and as one can imagine, his vote counted more than anyone else's.) Borrowing from Cistercian tradition, the new Norbertine abbots would now travel to Prémontré each year for what the order called a general chapter. There they could discuss important business and make institution-wide policy. The growth of this general chapter also provides a tidy snapshot of the rapid growth of the order overall. When Hugh convened the first one, in 1128, six abbots attended. A year later there were nine; two years later twelve; and three years later eighteen.

Importantly, the general chapter early on produced two essential documents that provided additional structure. One document was more operational and cultural in nature—a compilation of Premonstratensian customs and practices, the forerunner to its present-day Constitutions. The other built on the order's rule, outlining in detail its liturgical and prayer practices. Taken together, the new governance model and the defined common expectations provided some badly needed institutional direction, consistency and continuity while still permitting each foundation a generous amount of cultural independence. That flexibility helped ensure that, as the order spread, the individual abbeys could hew to the specific missions that gave rise to them in the first place. That's why, for instance, many of the French and Belgian communities "exhibited a strong monastic character and for a long time led a contemplative life," explains van den Hurk, while the Norbertine communities in Germany were far more geared to parish work from the outset. All told, this organizational fine-tuning began to establish the Premonstratensians, along with the Cistercians, as true forerunners of the modern religious order.

For Norbert personally, maybe the biggest change that came with his Magdeburg assignment, and the one that would shape the arc of the rest of his life, was his growing role as an intimate and counselor to Lothair. Not only did Norbert find himself back at court, but soon enough he would become a figure of formidable power.

Though Lothair hadn't really known Norbert before their encounter at Speyer, he evidently liked what he saw or the Magdeburg appointment would never have come to pass. But it seems clear the two men were in sympathy from the start. Within months of his consecration as archbishop, Norbert was summoned to Strasbourg by Lothair on court business. He would be similarly called to the court at Aachen, and his presence would repeatedly be required thereafter. More importantly, when in 1127 Lothair's rule was challenged by some powerful princes in the southern German region of Swabia, Norbert immediately excommunicated them. "Norbert unambiguously chose Lothair's side, in whose following he still regularly stayed," writes Grauwen. "Henceforth Norbert's influence on the king continually grew." More than that, events were about to make them blood partners.

IN FEBRUARY OF 1130, Pope Honorius died. No sooner was he cold than one faction of cardinals, aligned with the powerful Roman house of the Frangipani, hurriedly met to elect a successor, who took the name Innocent II. But a competing group of cardinals, backed by a competing Roman house— the Pierleonis—felt tricked by the pre-emptive vote. Just hours later those prelates convened a second election and chose one of their own, Peter Pierleoni, who took as his papal name Anacletus II. The Pierleonis were Italian nouveaux riches; the Frangipani represented old-line nobility. Because the Pierleonis had a stronger political hold on Rome itself, Innocent was forced to flee north. But the great battle between them, to determine who had the more legitimate claim on the papacy, was only beginning.

Their fight would primarily boil down to which side could secure the backing of Europe's most powerful rulers. In France, for instance, the king threw his support behind Innocent, largely due to the sway of Norbert's peer Bernard of Clairvaux. Similarly, both Innocent and Anacletus realized that to persuade Lothair and the Germans, they would first have to carry the day with the man who had the emperor's ear, Norbert. Norbert clearly understood his strategic position here. As it happened he was somewhat acquainted with both pope and antipope from interactions with them when they were cardinals, and it's believed Norbert's personal preference going in—at least strictly from a moral and spiritual standpoint—was for Innocent. Still, Norbert endeavored to learn as much as he could about both men before making up his mind. Toward that end he wrote to a pair of trusted Italian bishops to gain their views of both claimants, as well as what they knew of the circumstances surrounding the dueling elections. While Norbert's letters of outreach do not survive, the bishops' replies to him do, and in fact they have proven invaluable historical sources for the light they shed on the schism. In a nutshell, both Norbert's correspondents reassured him that Innocent was a good and worthy man, that his election was valid, and that Anacletus was widely considered a scheming pretender. They also assured Norbert that Anacletus had no real support beyond the Eternal City.

With that, Norbert readily persuaded Lothair to throw his support to Innocent and to help the pope gain acceptance throughout his realm. Then, that October, Lothair held a diet at Wuerzburg at which he publicly declared his position. The Church officials there excommunicated Anacletus, and with him the handful of German nobles in rebellion against Lothair. That was all tremendously helpful to Innocent, of course—but the fact remained that it was the antipope, Anacletus, who held St. Peter's while Innocent was still forced to conduct his campaign for legitimacy from a kind of roving exile. As part of that effort, Innocent and Lothair arranged to meet in March 1131 at a special council at Liege, in eastern Belgium, where with great fanfare they cemented their partnership—and where Lothair made a promise to take an army to Rome to remove Anacletus. After that meeting, Innocent went on to Laon for Holy Week, where he said Mass at the Norbertine abbey at St. Martin's and held an audience with Hugh of Fosse, conveying to him a papal bull that placed the Premonstratensian order under his special protection.

That papal show of respect was a telling sign of the key role Norbert played in this high-stakes drama. Equally telling was Anacletus' growing antipathy toward the archbishop. Early in the schismatic dispute Anacletus, hoping somehow to prevail with Lothair, had kept up a steady engagement with Norbert, treating him with caution but respect, alternating his expressions of inducement with calculated threats. But in the end, when Lothair made his choice clear, Anacletus actually excommunicated Norbert. The archbishop of Magdeburg tried his best to ignore what he considered an empty gesture from an illegitimate authority. Still, given the political reality of the situation— Anacletus remained on Peter's throne—it nevertheless must have given him pause. After all, as the dispute was far from resolved, Anacletus might yet prevail.

In October of 1131 hundreds of prelates from around the Holy Roman Empire gathered in Reims to consolidate their support of Innocent, who was in attendance, and to reiterate the excommunication of Anacletus. Norbert, there representing his liege, delivered to the pope a letter from Lothair formally reaffirming his earlier pledge to oust Anacletus. Lothair's intentions, while certainly noble, were not entirely altruistic. Restoring Innocent to his rightful place in Rome was only the first part of Lothair's plan. Once that was accomplished, he would have Innocent reciprocate by formally crowning him there as emperor at last, as popes traditionally had done. Such papal recognition would further strengthen Lothair's own claim to rule and maybe help him quash at last the residual opposition in his backyard.

FOR NORBERT IT HAD BEEN a year and a half of negotiations, nonstop travel and intense pressure—the twelfth-century version of shuttle diplomacy. By summer of 1132, as Lothair began to assemble his forces for the march to Italy, Norbert wanted nothing more than to return to Magdeburg and his "regular" duties. By now, however, he was one of the emperor's most valued confidantes; there was no way Lothair was going to leave Norbert behind, and the archbishop knew it. For this undertaking, in fact, Lothair conferred on Norbert the title of chancellor, formally acknowledging his influence in the imperial court. For his part, Pope Innocent, sensing how precipitous this whole enterprise would likely be, insisted Norbert come along as well. All of which put Norbert in a delicate, not to mention uniquely powerful, position. He was "the confidential agent of both of them," writes Grauwen. "With the king he represented the pope and with the pope he represented the king."

Lothair, meantime, had a problem, and it was a consequential one for a man preparing what was in essence a military incursion. Because of his ongoing opposition at home, Lothair was forced to hold back a large percentage of his available soldiers. The expeditionary army he mustered was considerably smaller than past German kings had taken to Italy. It's thought Lothair may have had as few as fifteen hundred troops for the difficult march across the Alps and any fighting that awaited them along the way.

And in fact, even before Lothair's army got out of Germany, blood was shed. Just one hundred miles south of Wuerzburg lay Augsburg, seat of the German resistance to the emperor. On the night the imperial forces arrived there, the atmosphere in Augsburg was tense. At the city market Lothair's soldiers got into an argument, then a scuffle, with some of the vendors. Rebel knights responded to the commotion. In the escalating heat of the moment each side believed it was being attacked by the other, and soon an all-out battle was under way. In time Lothair's army got the upper hand, and his troops proceeded to set fire to much of that prosperous city. What apparently began as a misunderstanding was becoming a slaughter. The bishop of Augsburg, who had been driven from his burning home, moved from combatant to combatant trying to stop the violence. Somehow in all the mayhem Norbert found his fellow prelate, by now in a state of shock, and took him under his own protection. Norbert implored Lothair to extend mercy to his enemies, but in this instance the vengeful monarch rebuffed his counselor.

Lothair's army continued on to Italy, where the emperor

met with Innocent to formulate a plan and then cautiously advanced south. As he did so, Anacletus sent representatives to try to change Lothair's mind. Stiffened by Norbert's own resolve, Lothair stayed firm. But Norbert had to keep up his guard, as the increasingly desperate antipope steadily dangled new propositions in front of Lothair as his army approached. Norbert found himself constantly toggling between Innocent's entourage and Lothair's camp to defuse each fresh stratagem.

Nearing Rome, Lothair slowed, knowing he did not really have the numbers to assault the city directly. Instead, he managed to come up from the southeast and secure a highly symbolic piece of it—St. John Lateran Basilica and the Lateran Palace. St. John Lateran is the oldest public church in the city and the official cathedral of the bishop of Rome. In late April 1133, with Lothair and Norbert at his side, Innocent II was installed there as pope. This was a major step toward legitimizing his authority, obviously. But once that was done, things fell into an awkward stasis: Anacletus continued to make proposals and buy time; Lothair felt he couldn't attack Anacletus head-on because he was outmanned; but Innocent was not going to crown Lothair emperor until he finished the job he'd come down to do: removing the antipope.

There things stood, and that's where they likely would have remained, until Norbert hit upon an acceptable way forward. In his compromise, Innocent *would* crown Lothair, but in the St. John Lateran Basilica. If it wasn't exactly St. Peter's, the venerable St. John Lateran setting was nonetheless a powerful symbol of papal authority. Lothair agreed.

So it was that on June 4, 1133, Innocent placed on Lothair's head the crown signifying his sovereignty over the Holy Roman Empire. Then, in the ensuing celebration, one final wrinkle made its unwelcome appearance. No doubt appreciating the strong hand he was holding, Lothair suddenly raised the possibility of reclaiming the right of investiture for bishops. His argument, Campbell writes, was that "it would strengthen the imperial authority and further cement the close relations existing between the pope and the emperor." Pope Innocent, appreciative of what Lothair had done for him and quite comfortable in their own relationship, didn't reject the idea out of hand. According to the standard account of this event, while there were numerous cardinals and bishops in attendance—many of them aghast at Lothair's out-of-the-blue request—only Norbert found the courage to stand and give voice to what everyone was thinking. "Father, what are you doing?" Norbert asked Innocent, with Lothair looking on. "To whom are you exposing the sheep entrusted to you only to have them torn to pieces?" Norbert argued that his two princes must set aside their own comity and the elation of the moment and instead consider the mayhem that would surely ensue if the investiture question was reopened. "Will you reduce to a maidservant the Church which was free when you received it?" he said. "The chair of Peter demands the deeds of Peter. I promised obedience to Peter and to you for the name of Christ, but if you do what is asked of you, I will speak against you in the face of the Church."

This remarkable scene comes down to us from *Vita A*. It represents such a bold, almost unimaginable rebuke of two powerful leaders that many historians have questioned whether it really happened. That skepticism might find inadvertent support in the fact that such a dramatic episode from Norbert's last years is not addressed at all in *Vita B*, which was written some years *after Vita A*.

For his part, Norbertine authority Grauwen concludes there is little question that "negotiations took place concerning the investiture right and Norbert certainly again played the role of mediator." While Grauwen concedes that the rendition in *Vita A* is definitely a "theatrical" take on how things played out (and that Norbert's brave speech was more likely an invention of his biographer), there's little doubt Norbert *was* largely responsible for defusing this momentary crisis and keeping Lothair faithful to the earlier Concordat of Worms.

What we know for a fact is that on the very day of Lothair's crowning Pope Innocent issued a decree personally thanking Norbert for all his support and political skill. "Your light has shone with ever increasing brightness, whilst your unfailing fidelity and devotion have become known not only to those around you but even to far distant nations," it said. "No fatigue, no threats, no flattery could prevent you from standing like an impregnable fortress against the tyranny of [Anacletus].... It is right, therefore, that the Apostolic See, which rejoices so greatly to have such a devoted son, should pay its debt of gratitude to you for all your services and labors and thus bind you even more closely to its service." In addition to the pretty words, the bull authorized Norbert's earlier request that the archdiocese of Magdeburg formally oversee the ecclesiastical affairs of Poland

and the region of Pomerania (territory that straddled what is today far northeast Germany and northwest Poland).

AT LAST LOTHAIR was poised to leave Rome. Before he did, he dispatched Norbert and Bernard to Anacletus one final time in the hope of striking some kind of a rapprochement, but that plan went nowhere. (Though he was the eventual victor, Innocent II would not actually occupy St. Peter's until Anacletus died in 1138.) Strictly in terms of its stated objectives, then, Lothair's expedition was rather less than a success. On the other hand, Innocent *had* gained widespread acceptance as the "true" head of the Church, and in the process Lothair had managed to consolidate his own imperial authority. And as for Norbert, it can be said that he had profited as well. He had formally gained the control he had sought for the See of Magdeburg over his eastern frontier. More importantly, he had—whether by his own plan or by happenstance or providence—fulfilled the role of high-level statesman he'd seemed destined to play when he was still that ambitious cleric apprenticing in Frederick's court. Throughout Europe Norbert was recognized and respected, not only as a dedicated man of God but as a skilled, statesmanlike servant to his monarch.

The price for that achievement, however, was high. By the time the army decamped in June of 1133, it had been on the move for almost a year. Not only was Norbert suffering from general exhaustion but he could feel his essential health ebbing.

He was at this point a man likely in his middle to late fifties—and one whose body had logged more long, and hard, miles than any in Europe. Now he was sick, which only made his desire to get back to Magdeburg all the more acute.

But he also knew that Lothair had other plans in mind. It would hardly be a straight line home.

CHAPTER 10

THE LEGACY

By late August of 1133 the imperial army had marched its way back to Bavaria, and in early September Lothair's court arrived in Wuerzburg for a celebration and another diet to tend to some pending Church matters. The entourage made several other stops before rolling into Cologne in time for Christmas. From there it was on to Aachen for the feast of Epiphany, then across Germany to Goslar, in Lower Saxony, in February. At long last Magdeburg was in reach; Goslar is just fifty miles to the west. But the grueling return of the army and Lothair's "victory lap" had consumed another eight months, by which point Norbert was so debilitated that he was bed-bound. It's not known with certainty, but based on where Norbert had been and the progression of his symptoms through the end of 1133 and into 1134, it's highly likely that he contracted malaria when he was in Rome—a place notorious through history for that deadly, mosquito-borne disease.

Carried the remaining leg of his journey, Norbert finally re-entered his episcopal home on Ash Wednesday. His servants and clerics brought to Norbert's sickbed the work that had piled up during his nearly two-year absence. But now Norbert was in constant pain and had virtually no energy. Nevertheless, he did his best to deal with various priorities, from managing important building projects to endeavoring to arrange for his own successor at Magdeburg—a person he hoped might have both the courage and protection to carry on his reform agenda. He did manage to get on his feet for the occasional short visit, particularly to see his confreres at St. Mary's. And he seemed especially intent on carrying out many of the archbishop's usual duties for the Lenten season, even though he was in no real condition to do so. "By an almost superhuman effort Norbert went to the cathedral on Maundy Thursday to bless the holy oils," writes Campbell, "and again on Easter Sunday, April 15, when, seated in a chair, he celebrated the High Mass."

As it turned out, it would be his final liturgy. Soon after, Norbert slid into a pronounced decline. He sent word back to Prémontré for Hugh to come, but there would not be time. On June 6, 1134, in the company of the devoted Evermode and the St. Mary's canons, Norbert offered his colleagues a final blessing and then expired.

NORBERT, AS WE KNOW, was a man of ironies. One of the most confounding of these was the fact that, for someone with such a richly deserved reputation for peacemaking, he had a knack for leaving controversy in his wake. Whether as a halfhearted subdeacon, a zealous "convert" trying to tell other clergy how to live, a self-anointed preacher, a fiery Church reformer, an iconoclastic founder of an iconoclastic new order, a hardheaded archbishop or a clearheaded papal counselor, Norbert always managed to throw off sparks. Now, even in death, he unwittingly prompted a nasty fight.

When it came time to determine the disposition of Norbert's earthly remains, an impassioned dispute broke out between the canons at the Magdeburg cathedral and the Norbertines at St. Mary's. Logically enough, the group from the cathedral argued that of course Norbert would be interred in the cathedral, the traditional resting place of the city's metropolitans. However, the St. Mary's community, led by Evermode, countered that Norbert should reside amid the religious community that he had founded—an institution so intimately associated with the man that his followers were called Norbertines. Besides, argued Evermode, Norbert had said many times that that was his wish. As there was but one corpse available, a compromise was unlikely. And in fact the conflict remained so emotional and intractable that at last it went up to Lothair himself for resolution. In the end, the emperor ruled that Norbert would be entombed at St. Mary's, at the Church of Our Lady, there to remain in eternal communion with his beloved confreres.

Norbert would have been dismayed by the unseemly controversy as to his remains. On the other hand, he was surely gratified to live long enough to know that his religious order was on firm ground. Not only would it survive him, it was already thriving. Because of his vision and political wits, the Premonstratensians were now robust enough, and firmly enough rooted, that they had clearly crossed some invisible threshold: They no longer needed Norbert as the sole piston driving their continued growth.

At the time of Norbert's death in 1134, there were already one hundred or more abbeys and other Premonstratensian foundations in existence, and that surge would continue unabated for a century. This growth was not just about numbers but geographical reach. The Premonstratensian presence would always be strongest in the core areas where Norbert had been personally active—certain regions of Germany, France and Belgium—but it took strong root as well in Spain, Austria, Hungary, England, Scotland, Ireland and what are now the Czech Republic and Slovakia. Norbertine foundations would also push south into Italy and north into Scandinavia. The order spread with the Crusades into the Holy Land; it went to Poland, to Denmark, to Riga in modern-day Latvia. Given the highly transitory nature of some of these early foundations and the spotty documentation of that age, it is impossible to know with precision how many existed at any given time. But some published estimates said that by the middle of the fourteenth century—just two hundred years after Norbert's death—there were more than one thousand institutions of his order extant. That figure is likely exaggerated, but not by a lot. Norbertine scholars, having scoured available records, suggest that at the order's peak there were upward of seven hundred abbeys and subsidiary institutions. In the end, the exact number matters less than the obvious point: the Norbertine order would stand as one of the most robust examples of early Catholic renewal of religious life.

And at the center of that stunning evolution, Prémontré,

the once modest community carved out of the French wilderness, would become a grand manor to rival that of kings—a palatial compound with ornate buildings and elegantly tree-lined allées, its farms and gardens and orchards stretching out in all directions. Year after year saw an ever-growing number of Norbertine abbots, their donkeys and horses exchanged for fine carriages, journey there for general chapters. They came to conduct Norbertine business, yes, but in a sense these annual pilgrimages also paid tribute to the influential outpost that the once-humble mother abbey had become.

Paradoxically, as the order continued its rise, the personal renown of its founder began to wane. A big reason for this—yet another irony—was because Norbert's own example inspired the next generation of charismatic holy men, including the mendicant reformers Dominic and Francis, who would become considerably better known than their forebear. Some said another factor was that the Premonstratensians, with their relatively decentralized structure and continuing preoccupation in those first generations with managing their growth, were not especially aggressive in advocating for Norbert's memory or sainthood.

But as much as anything this state of affairs was simply a product of passing time. And as those decades, and then centuries, rolled by, the once-famous Norbert seemed destined to fade from public memory—until, that is, the Protestant Reformation arose to shake the Catholic Church to its core. As we know, one of the many Catholic doctrines that came under assault from Protestant leaders was the idea of the real presence of Christ in the Eucharist. As the Church mounted its counter-Reformation efforts, Norbert's work in support of the Eucharist and his role in quashing an earlier outbreak of heresy in Antwerp were now remembered and held up in example. Slowly his life story began to be revived, and with that revival came a fresh push for his sainthood. Norbert would be canonized by Pope Gregory XIII in 1582, his feast day to be observed on June 6, the anniversary of his death in Magdeburg.

Through those intervening generations, between death and canonization, it had been self-evident to many observers that Norbert, with his litany of genuine accomplishments in the service of the Church, had more than earned his seat among the communion of saints. Though an admitted admirer of Norbert, Herman of Tournai was probably not far off the mark when, fairly soon after Norbert's death, he would write: "There has been no one since the time of the apostles who in such a brief space of time has acquired for Christ so many imitators of the perfect life through his institute." Yet from our modern vantage point, living in a public relations age, we can especially appreciate one more Norbert irony—that he finally got his due from Rome less for what he actually did than because his story proved so useful to the Church at a major crisis point. Rome in essence "spun" Norbert's story for its own purposes. It focused almost exclusively on his reverence for the Eucharist and his tenacious defense of Catholic dogma—both undeniable hallmarks of Norbert's record—to the virtual exclusion of all the other priorities that characterized his busy life: the reform agenda, the peacemaking, the apostolic model, the Gospel values and service to the common man, the establishment of a major religious order, the high-level statesmanship. Yet that redefining of Norbert was so successful that, even now, it is challenging to make out the "real" saint through the mists of time. "Only in 1582 was Norbert canonized, and from then onwards his cult and iconography developed," observes Grauwen. "All this is of no historical importance; on the contrary, this evolution has rather misconstrued and hidden the real image of Norbert. Norbert was a strong personality of the twelfth century and has to be studied as a prince of the Church at that time. How later centuries have tried to fit his character into the popular pattern of the ideal of sanctity may be of interest for the study of hagiography but it does not add anything more to the true historical knowledge of his personality."

Whatever Rome's motivations, its rediscovery and elevation of Norbert did reawaken his following. We know this in large part because it was throughout this era that Norbert suddenly becomes a focal point of Catholic artwork—paintings, engravings, sculpture. Invariably in these he is depicted holding the monstrance (another irony, since the vessel for Eucharistic adoration wouldn't come into common use until centuries after Norbert had died). In many other depictions Norbert is subduing Tanchelm under his foot—even though the heretic had died almost a decade before Norbert arrived in Antwerp. But as with all religious art, literalness was utterly beside the point; these were pieces for inspiration and edification. Examples of this Norbertine iconography abound, but it will suffice to note that no less than the Flemish master Peter Paul Rubens made celebrated paintings of Norbert featuring both the Eucharistic and anti-heresy motifs.

One last twist: No sooner was Norbert's reputation on the rebound when the fortunes of the Premonstratensian order at large were sliding toward what would become centuries of travail. The earliest headwinds came from an array of unrelated sources: the spread of Islam, the rise of the popular Dominican and Franciscan orders, the great bubonic plague of the mid-fourteenth century. But it was the great Reformation movement that delivered the most brutal blow, nearly halving the number of Norbertine institutions throughout Europe as abbeys were burned, confiscated, closed or converted to Protestant denominations. Then came the French Revolution in the late eighteenth century and Napoleon's suppression of religious communities in the early nineteenth, which, in combination, nearly finished the job. After these waves of devastation, any canvass of Norbertine abbeys would have been much simpler; so few remained that they could be counted on two hands, with some fingers left over.

And yet...just when it seemed the proud Premonstratensian order was going under for a final time, the White Fathers managed to rally in the late nineteenth century. Initiative by initiative, house by house, a community that had largely gone underground began to return to the light and determinedly gave rise to a renaissance that would carry the order into the modern world. All those centuries later, Norbert's inspiring example had been strong enough to sustain his namesake community in the face of so much tragedy and atrocity—just as it would sustain the Norbertines against the shocks of the twentieth century: a world war, then another, the rise of fascism and communism, the rise of consumerism, the threat of nuclear annihilation and so much more. Through it all, the Norbertines endured—smaller in numbers now but broader in reach; repurposed in many ways but still fully committed to the values and principles that their founder personally set forth in the woods of Prémontré. That resilience would, of necessity, become part of the order's DNA. Indeed, at some point in its history, when it had enough age and confidence to back it up, the Premonstratensians adopted a telling motto from Augustine: "Ever ancient, ever new."

In modern times the Norbertines would export their venerable message around the world. Today there are well over one hundred functioning communities, most located in Europe but also to be found in Australia, India, Brazil and the United States. In fact, the story of the Norbertines' coming to America is a particularly illuminating example of how Norbert's entrepreneurial spirit was never truly extinguished.

Berne Abbey, located south of Amsterdam, was one of the foundations established in that initial Premonstratensian "Big Bang." It dates to 1134, the year of Norbert's death. (Legend has it that its existence owes to a Dutch knight who, in the duress of battle, plunged into the Maas River to save himself and promised God he would establish an abbey if he survived. He did.) Berne would become one of the order's more influential abbeys, surviving centuries of war, suppressions and dislocations. Then in the late nineteenth century its influence crossed the Atlantic. Answering a call for help from America, a young Berne confrere named Bernard Pennings was dispatched to Wisconsin to counter a rogue priest who had gained support among Dutch and Belgian settlers in the Door County region, just northeast of Green Bay. That job accomplished, Pennings stayed on to establish a foundation in the fledgling settlement of De Pere, along a picturesque bend in the Fox River. That humble out-post would blossom into a large abbey and, in turn, found other Norbertine communities in the States—in Paoli, Pennsylvania; in Albuquerque, New Mexico; in Middletown, Delaware; and in Jackson, Mississippi. St. Norbert Abbey would further come to welcome confreres from the abbey of Csorna (Hungary) who founded St. Michael's Abbey in Orange County, California. Pennings—in 1925 he was appointed abbot—would also go on to found and lead St. Norbert College in De Pere, the only traditional baccalaureate institution in the order's long history. (In the Middle Ages, though, the Norbertines *did* establish esteemed theological schools in some of the great universities of Europe.) A highly respected liberal arts institution, St. Norbert College advances the Norbertine mission in many ways—including, in a nod to the Premonstratensian tradition of great libraries, its creation and operation of the Center for Norbertine Studies, a global repository of the order's culture, literature, history, art and artifacts.

AS THIS BOOK IS BEING written, the Order of Premon-stratensians is on the verge of celebrating its nine-hundred-year jubilee. So as one considers the legacy of St. Norbert, it must be acknowledged that his greatest impact was the founding of an institution that has faithfully served countless millions of people, around the world—Catholics and non-Catholics alike whose lives would have been greatly diminished without the Norbertine presence. Such endurance by *any* institution is only possible if the founder's principles were genuinely worthy and his or her life an example that continues to inspire.

Indeed, like any transcendent figure, Norbert was not just a person of his time but a person for *all* times. That was his genius, and his gift to us. If in the twenty-first century we seek lessons to take away from his eventful life, we should think less about the twelfth-century man than about the timeless principles that guided and spurred him. If Norbert was a wandering preacher today, it's not hard to imagine the instruction he would offer us: Put your faith into action. Commit yourself to helping others. Be a peacemaker in your life. Use the talents God has given you not just to improve the world around you but to improve the Church you are part of—even if, at times, that means pointing out its imperfections and inequities. Trust in God, and trust in yourself to do his work. Then get on with it.

When in late 1626 the recovery party from Prague left Magdeburg with Norbert's remains, they stopped to overwinter at a convent in the village of Doksany, in what is now the Czech Republic. In commemoration of the sacred occasion of its patron's translation, the community of nuns there planted a ginkgo tree just beyond the convent walls. The convent, like the order itself, grew and then shrank, even to the point of extinction when it was suppressed under Emperor Joseph II in the eighteenth century. But the convent, reopened after the fall of communism, is still there, along with eight or so dedicated women who eke out an existence through a variety of means, including the stitching of beautiful vestments for priests.

Still there, too, is the ginkgo—now such a magnificent specimen that it is more than one hundred feet tall, with a trunk so massive that five of the Doksany nuns could ring it with their arms extended and still not touch hands. Four centuries old, the ginkgo is a formidable and apt symbol—of strength, of beauty, of fidelity, of endurance, of rebirth and renewal, its leaves dropping all at once in the fall and then regenerating with the coming spring.

Ever ancient, ever new.

KEY EVENTS IN NORBERT'S LIFE

ca. 1075 Born into noble family in or near Gennep, in present-day the Netherlands

MID–1080s TO EARLY 1100s Undergoes formal education, in training for the priesthood
Becomes subdeacon in chapter of canons at the collegiate church of St. Victor's in Xanten, Germany
Joins court of Archbishop Frederick in Cologne as chaplain
Joins court of Holy Roman Emperor Henry V, works in chancery and royal chapel

1110–11 Participates in imperial march to Rome amid Investiture Controversy, witnesses Henry's abusive treatment of Pope Paschal II

1113 Is said to refuse bishopric of Cambrai, in France—possibly in reaction to ill-treatment of Paschal

1115 Has a dramatic conversion experience, pledges his life to God
Is ordained as a deacon and priest on the same day

1116–18 Fails in effort to reform Xanten canons
Undertakes a period of intensive prayer and seclusion, trying to discern God's plan for him
Commits to follow the example of Christ's apostles, begins itinerant ministry

1118   Faces formal accusations of unsanctioned clerical behavior
at Church council in Fritzlar, Germany
Gives up all his worldly goods and possessions
Secures permission from Pope Gelasius II to be a
wandering preacher

1119   Begins preaching full-time, primarily in northern France
and Belgium
Sees several of his exhausted companions die during
Holy Week in Valenciennes, France
Reunites with old friend Burchard, bishop of Cambrai,
and meets his future lieutenant, Hugh of Fosse
Along road in Reims, France, meets Bartholomew, bishop
of Laon
After death of Gelasius, secures permission from
Callixtus II to continue preaching

1120   Spends winter of 1119–20 in Laon
Is asked to reform chapter of canons at St. Martin's in
Laon, but they balk at the severity of his proposed
agenda
Is invited by Bartholomew to establish his own religious
community
Selects a remote wooded site near Laon, called Prémontré
Begins recruiting confreres and building the community,
which includes canons but also sisters, lay men and
lay women

1121   Oversees rapid growth of Prémontré
Travels to Cologne to secure relics, finds remains
of St. Gereon

Establishes second foundation, at Floreffe, in Belgium
Adopts Rule of Augustine for his community
Conducts first profession of vows at Christmas—the
    beginning of the Premonstratensian order

1122   Collaborates with Godfrey of Cappenberg, paving way for
    first Norbertine foundations in Germany

1123   Goes to Antwerp, Belgium to counter heresies of Tanchelm
Establishes St. Michael's of Antwerp as a Norbertine
    foundation

1124   Establishes St. Martin's in Laon as a Norbertine foundation

1126   Travels to Rome; receives papal bull from Pope Honorius II
    formally recognizing Premonstratensian order; said to
    hear voice calling him to "Parthenopolis" (Magdeburg,
    Germany) bishopric
Miraculously heals blind woman during Mass at
    Wuerzburg, Germany
Leaves Prémontré for last time
At Diet of Speyer, is drafted as archbishop of Magdeburg

1127   Upon vote of order's superiors, appoints Hugh of Fosse
    first abbot general of Premonstratensian order

1128   Returns to Xanten to consecrate parts of new cathedral

1129   Makes St. Mary's in Magdeburg a Norbertine abbey
Survives several assassination attempts by opponents
    of his reforms

1130	Persuades his emperor, Lothair III, to support Innocent II over antipope Anacletus II in papal schism
1132	Named chancellor by Lothair, accompanies imperial army in march to Rome to oust Anacletus
1133	Succeeds in seeing Innocent installed as pope and Lothair crowned as emperor; plays major role in averting new investiture crisis
1134	Returns to Magdeburg after a nearly two-year absence Dies on June 6 after long illness; there are already one hundred Norbertine foundations in existence
1582	Is canonized by the Church
1627	Remains are "translated" from Magdeburg to Strahov Abbey in Prague
2021	The Order Praemonstratensis—the Norbertines— celebrates the nine hundredth anniversary of the first professions to the order

A NOTE ON THE SOURCES

The two primary resources for anyone studying the life of Norbert of Xanten are a pair of connected biographies produced by his Premonstratensian followers within a few decades of the founder's death in 1134. These are *Vita Norberti A* (or *Vita A*) and *Vita Norberti B* (*Vita B*). The order's scholars believe *Vita A* was written first and apparently came from Norbert's German colleagues. *Vita B*, which came a decade or two later, seems written from the perspective of the French Norbertines. It tracks closely with the *Vita A* narrative but is considerably longer, its authors having fleshed out the original biographical sketch with more scriptural citations, moralizing anecdotes and commentary.

The most comprehensive modern scholarship on Norbert has been done by the Rev. Wilfried Grauwen, O. Praem., a member of the Postel Abbey community in Belgium. He has devoted much of his scholarly career to unearthing all he could about Norbert's life and times, and then bringing a sharp analytic eye to what he found.

In 1978 he published a detailed look at Norbert from the time he was named archbishop of Magdeburg in 1126 until his death. Later Grauwen would turn his attention to the pre-Magdeburg years, work encompassing Norbert's family background and character, court experiences, preaching career, and the founding and cultivating of Prémontré and the early Norbertine order. Grauwen produced several dozen chapters on these events. I was grateful to be able to draw heavily from both sources.

Another internationally respected Norbertine authority is the Rev. Theodore Antry, O. Praem., at the Daylesford Abbey community in Pennsylvania. He has produced countless essays and presentations and translated as many scholarly articles about Norbert from European historians and theologians. He provided this trove to me, which was immensely helpful. So too was a dual, side-by-side translation he made of *Vita A* and *Vita B*.

The Rev. Dominique-Marie Dauzet, O. Praem., is a writer and historian based at Mondaye Abbey in France. He is writing a book about the history of the Norbertines, and he was kind enough to share with me his first chapter, on Norbert and the order's foundation at Prémontré.

The Right Rev. Benjamin Mackin, O. Praem, was abbot of St. Norbert Abbey in De Pere, Wisconsin, from 1982 until 1994. At some point he was asked to convey his thoughts about Norbert's life and work to the abbey's novices, to help in their formation. Those talks formed the basis for a lengthy treatise on Norbert. While never published, that work from Mackin is unusually insightful about Norbert.

Here follows a list of key published sources I relied on. All these publications, as well as the resources cited above and many more, are available at the Center for Norbertine Studies at St. Norbert College.

Antry, Theodore J., and Carol Neel, editors. *Norbert and Early Norbertine Spirituality.* Mahwah, New Jersey, Paulist, 2007.

Ardura, Bernard. *The Order of Prémontré: History and Spirituality.* Translated by Edward Hagman. De Pere, Wisconsin, Paisa, 1995.

Campbell, Hamish. *Saint Norbert: Founder of the Order of Prémontré, Apostle of Peace.* Published by the Norbertine community of Storrington, England, 1984.

Cushing, Kathleen G. *Reform and the Papacy in the Eleventh Century: Spirituality and Social Change.* Manchester, Manchester University Press, 2005.

Fried, Johannes. *The Middle Ages.* Translated by Peter Lewis. Cambridge, Massachusetts, Belknap/Harvard, 2015.

Grauwen, Wilfried. *Norbert, Archbishop of Magdeburg.* Brussels, Academie, 1978. Note: This has been published in several languages, but not in English. An unpublished English translation is available at the Center for Norbertine Studies.

Kirkfleet, Cornelius James. *History of Saint Norbert: Founder of the Norbertine Order, Apostle of the Blessed Sacrament, Archbishop of Magdeburg.* St. Louis, B. Herder, 1916.

Louthan, Howard. *Converting Bohemia: Force and Persuasion in the Catholic Reformation.* Cambridge, England, Cambridge University Press, 2009.

Melville, Gert. *The World of Medieval Monasticism: Its History and Forms of Life.* Dubuque, Iowa, Cistercian, 2016.

Petit, Francois. *Spirituality of the Premonstratensians: The Twelfth and Thirteenth Centuries.* Edited by Carol Neel, translated by Victor Szczurek. Collegeville, Minnesota, Liturgical Press, 2011.

Saint Norbert Abbey. Untitled history of St. Norbert Abbey and St. Norbert College. Published by St. Norbert Abbey, De Pere, Wisconsin, 1936.

suor Santa, Dino. *The Spirituality of St. Norbert of Xanten*. Translated by Edward C. Stibili. A privately published English-language version (1959) is available at the Center for Norbertine Studies.

Toynbee, Arnold J. *A Study of History* (abridged). New York, Oxford, 1946.

Vanasse, Roman R., ed. *Reclaiming Our Norbertine Heritage*. Published by St. Norbert Abbey, De Pere, Wisconsin, 1995.

Van den Hurk, A. W. *Norbert of Gennep and His Order*. Translated by W. J. Smeets and R. Pasensie. Averbode, Belgium, Altiora-Averbode, 1984.

ACKNOWLEDGEMENTS

In the Introduction I recognize a number of scholars, academics and Norbertines who assisted me in the research and writing of this book. But I would be remiss if I didn't also thank a number of St. Norbert College associates and others who helped bring this project to fruition.

Susan Allen, who shepherded my presidential communications for many years, did her usual masterful job in editing the manuscript. Susan is that rare editor whose ear is as sharp as her eye, and I am grateful for her suggestions and many improvements. Proofreader Gretchen Panzer backstopped her, while Laura Treichel and Nick Patton were responsible for the book's elegant look and production. Meantime, I send special thanks to my dear friend Amy Sorenson, chief of staff to President Brian Bruess, for all her usual assistance, courtesies and catches.

The talented artist Martin Erspamer, a Benedictine brother at the St. Meinrad Archabbey community in southern Indiana, created the striking cover and related illustrations that grace the book. Much appreciated, Brother Martin.

Finally, I wish to thank my wife, Deb, who is not only a wonderful life partner but a first reader of great tact and firm opinion. I've never quite figured out how she manages to be right so often, but I'm glad she is.

St. Norbert College

St. Norbert College, a Catholic, Norbertine liberal arts college in
De Pere, Wisconsin, was founded in 1898 by the Rev. Bernard Pennings,
O. Praem., a priest of Berne Abbey in Holland. Pennings, sent to the
United States as a missionary priest, became prior of the first Norbertine
community to be established in North America. In 1925, he became first
abbot of the new St. Norbert Abbey. St. Norbert College remains the
abbey's primary apostolate and the only Norbertine institution of
higher education in the world.

Center for Norbertine Studies

The Center for Norbertine Studies is the international locus for Norbertine
studies. A collaborative partnership of the college and the Norbertine order,
the center works with Norbertines around the world to explore ways in which
the order's rich heritage can continue to inform and help shape spiritual,
intellectual and cultural life in today's global community. The center fosters
opportunities for undergraduate and graduate scholarship, collaboration
between Norbertine houses throughout the world, cross-cultural interaction,
and international exchange. The center, located on the campus of
St. Norbert College in De Pere, Wisconsin, was established in 2006.

Made in the USA
Middletown, DE
22 May 2021